THE LANGUAGE GYM

THE LANGUAGE GYM

ABSOLUTE BEGINNER ARABIC SENTENCE BUILDERS

A lexicogrammar approach

PRIMARY

BOOK ZERO

Copyright © G. Conti and D. Viñales

This book is fully photocopiable but may not be scanned and shared

Imprint: Language Gym

About the authors

Yusuf Amejee has taught for over 5 years, in schools in France and the UK. He is a Teach First Ambassador and currently lives in London, England. He is fluent in three languages and is currently learning a few more. Besides teaching, Yusuf has an avid interest in language learning, history, educational technology and classical Arabic. He is currently working on developing digital platforms for learning both modern and classical Arabic. He is also a passionate traveller and a fitness enthusiast. Currently, Yusuf has been implementing the E.P.I method both privately and at his school Bolder Academy.

Wael Rashwan has been a teacher for the last 28 years, 18 of which have been in Saudi Arabia. He is a skilled and highly experienced teacher of Arabic, and has specialised as a first and second language for both IGCSE and IB curricula. In addition, Wael has also taught in several centres that teach Arabic for non Arabic speakers, such as Berlitz where he taught diplomats and senior employees. Wael is currently a teacher of Arabic at the British International School in Riyadh.

Simona Gravina has taught for 15 years, in schools in Italy and the UK, both in state and independent settings. She lives in Glasgow, Scotland. She is fluent in three languages and gets by in a few more. Simona is, besides a teacher, a mum, a bookworm, a passionate traveller and a fitness enthusiast. In the last couple of years she has been testing and implementing E.P.I. in one of the top Independent schools in Scotland, St Aloysius'College, where she is currently Modern Languages Curriculum Leader in the Junior School.

Stefano Pianigiani is a Language Development Leader, teaching Primary and Secondary pupils at Appleton Academy in Bradford, England. He is an ECT mentor and SCITT MFL tutor for Exceed Academies Trust. He is fluent in four languages, and has taught Spanish, Italian and French all the way from Primary to A Level. He has a wide cultural experience having studied and lived in Italy, Spain and England. Stefano has completed his MA in Education at Leeds Trinity University. He is an enthusiastic educator and fervent creator of resources who has fully embraced Dr Conti's teaching from its very origins.

Gianfranco Conti taught for 25 years at schools in Italy, the UK and in Kuala Lumpur, Malaysia. He has also been a university lecturer, holds a Master's degree in Applied Linguistics and a PhD in metacognitive strategies as applied to second language writing. He is now an author, a popular independent educational consultant and a professional development provider. He has co-authored the best-selling and influential book for world languages teachers, "The Language Teacher Toolkit", "Breaking the sound barrier: Teaching learners how to listen", in which he puts forth his Listening As Modelling methodology and "Memory: what every language teacher should know". Last but not least, Gianfranco has created the instructional approach known as E.P.I. (Extensive Processing Instruction).

Dylan Viñales has taught for 15 years, in schools in Bath, Beijing and Kuala Lumpur in state, independent and international settings. He lives in Kuala Lumpur. He is fluent in five languages, and gets by in several more. Dylan is, besides a teacher, a professional development provider, specialising in E.P.I., metacognition, teaching languages through music (especially ukulele) and cognitive science. In the last five years, together with Dr Conti, he has driven the implementation of E.P.I. in one of the top international schools in the world: Garden International School. Dylan authors an influential blog on modern language pedagogy in which he supports the teaching of languages through E.P.I.

DEDICATION

For my lucky bird Huma
- Yusuf

For my family
- Wael

For my daughter Giulia
-Simona

For Skyla & Tessa
-Stefano

For Catrina
-Gianfranco

For Ariella & Leonard
-Dylan

Acknowledgements

Creating a book is a time-consuming yet rewarding endeavour.

Yusuf would like to thank his wife Huma, for all her encouragement and support as well as his students Ibby, Nura, Huda` Zakariyya and all those who actively engaged with the testing and gave feedback on the tasks. Huge gratitude also to Dylan for being an inspiring and motivating colleague.

Secondly, Yusuf would like to thank his colleagues and pupils at Bolder Academy, for all the contributions and advice in testing the tasks.

Our sincere gratitude to all the people involved in the recording of the Listening audio files: Huma, Nura and Naheed. Your energy, enthusiasm and passion comes across clearly in every recording and is the reason why the listening sections are such a successful and engaging resource, according to the many students who have been alpha and beta testing the book.

Thanks to Flaticon.com and Mockofun.com for providing access to a limitless library of engaging icons, clipart and images which we have used to make this book more user-friendly than any other Sentence Builders predecessor, with a view to be as engaging as possible for primary level students.

Our heartfelt gratitude to Abdul Rahman Alsaid for his invaluable assistance in bringing this Arabic language book to life. His meticulous proofreading and insightful content suggestions have played a pivotal role in shaping this project and we are grateful to him for so generously lending us his time and expertise.

Finally, our gratitude to the MFL Twitterati for their ongoing support of E.P.I. and the Sentence Builders book series. In particular a shoutout to our team of incredible educators who helped in checking all the units: Rahmeh Ghunmat, Sara Mustafa, Chirine El Hachache, Nicholas Ainsworth & Maha Jibreel.

It is thanks to the time, patience, professionalism and detailed feedback from these friends and colleagues that we have been able to produce such a refined and highly accurate product.

Shukran lakum!
Yusuf, Wael, Gianfranco & Dylan

Introduction

Hello and welcome to the first Sentence Builders workbook designed for Primary aged children, designed to be an accompaniment to a Arabic Extensive Processing Instruction course. The book has come about out of necessity, because such a resource did not previously exist.

What's inside?

This book: **ABSOLUTE BEGINNER ARABIC SENTENCE BUILDERS** A lexicogrammar approach PRIMARY - BOOK ZERO is meant as an introduction to BOOK ONE. The purpose of this book is for students to learn the alphabet, practise reading and writing the Arabic script and communicate basic phrases about their name, age and how they are feeling. This book is primarily aimed at students with zero level of Arabic but can also be used to consolidate previous knowledge.

How to use this book if you have bought into our E.P.I. approach

This book was originally designed as a resource to use in conjunction with our E.P.I. approach and teaching strategies. Our course favours flooding comprehensible input, organising content by communicative functions and related constructions, and a big focus on reading and listening as modelling. The aim of this book is to empower the beginner learner with linguistic tools - high-frequency structures and vocabulary - useful for real-life communication. Since, in a typical E.P.I. unit of work, aural and oral work play a huge role, this book should not be viewed as the ultimate E.P.I. coursebook, but rather as a **useful resource** to **complement** your Listening-As-Modelling and Speaking activities.

Sentence Builders – Online Versions

Please note that all these sentence builders will be available on the Language Gym website, available to download, editable and optimised for displaying in the classroom, via the Locker Room section (only available with a Language Gym subscription).

◀◝)) Audio tracks

Whenever you see an audio icon, it means that there is some kind of listening exercise or opportunity. These audios have been made by a native speaker team and can be accessed, free of charge, at: **language-gym.com**, in the **AUDIO** section. This section can be freely accessed without a subscription.

How to use this book if you are not already an EPI teacher

If you would like to learn about E.P.I. you could read one of the authors' blogs. The definitive guide is Dr Conti's "Patterns First – How I Teach Lexicogrammar" which can be found on his blog (www.gianfrancoconti.com). There are also blogs on Dylan's wordpress site (mrvinalesmfl.wordpress.com) such as "Using sentence builders to reduce (everyone's) workload and create more fluent linguists" which can be read to get teaching ideas and to learn how to structure a course, through all the stages of E.P.I.

Examples of E.P.I. activities and games to play in class, based on MARS EARS sequence, can be found in Simona's padlet (https://en-gb.padlet.com/simograv/svi55fluxeolisi9) "MFL Teaching based on E.P.I. approach, Videos and blogs, Sample activities from Modelling to Spontaneity". These can be used to model tasks.

The book "Breaking the Sound Barrier: Teaching Learners how to Listen" by Gianfranco Conti and Steve Smith, provides a detailed description of the approach and of the listening and speaking activities you can use in synergy with the present book.

We do hope that you and your students will find this book useful and enjoyable.

Yusuf, Wael, Gianfranco & Dylan

Table of Contents

ALPHABET GUIDE

The following few pages are reference for teachers to consult in the teaching of the alphabet should they need it.

تمر	ت ـت ة/ة	بيت	ب ـبـ ب	أسد	أ ا أَ
حمام	حـ ـحـ ح	جمل	جـ ـجـ ج	ثلاجة	ثـ ـثـ ث
ذبابة	ذ ـذ ـذ	دائرة	د ـد ـد	خروف	خـ ـخـ خ

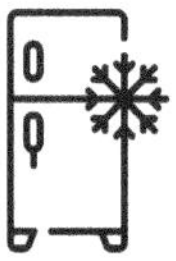

	ر		ز		س
	ر		ز		سـ
رمان	ر	زرافة	ز	سمكة	ـس

	ش		ص		ض
	ش		صـ		ضـ
شمعة	ش	صاروخ	ص	ضابط	ض

	ط		ظ		ع
	ط		ظ		ـع
طائرة	ط	ظرف	ظ	عين	ـعـ

	غ		ف		ق
	غ		ف		ق
غسالة	غ	فراشة	ف	قلم	ق

THE LANGUAGE GYM

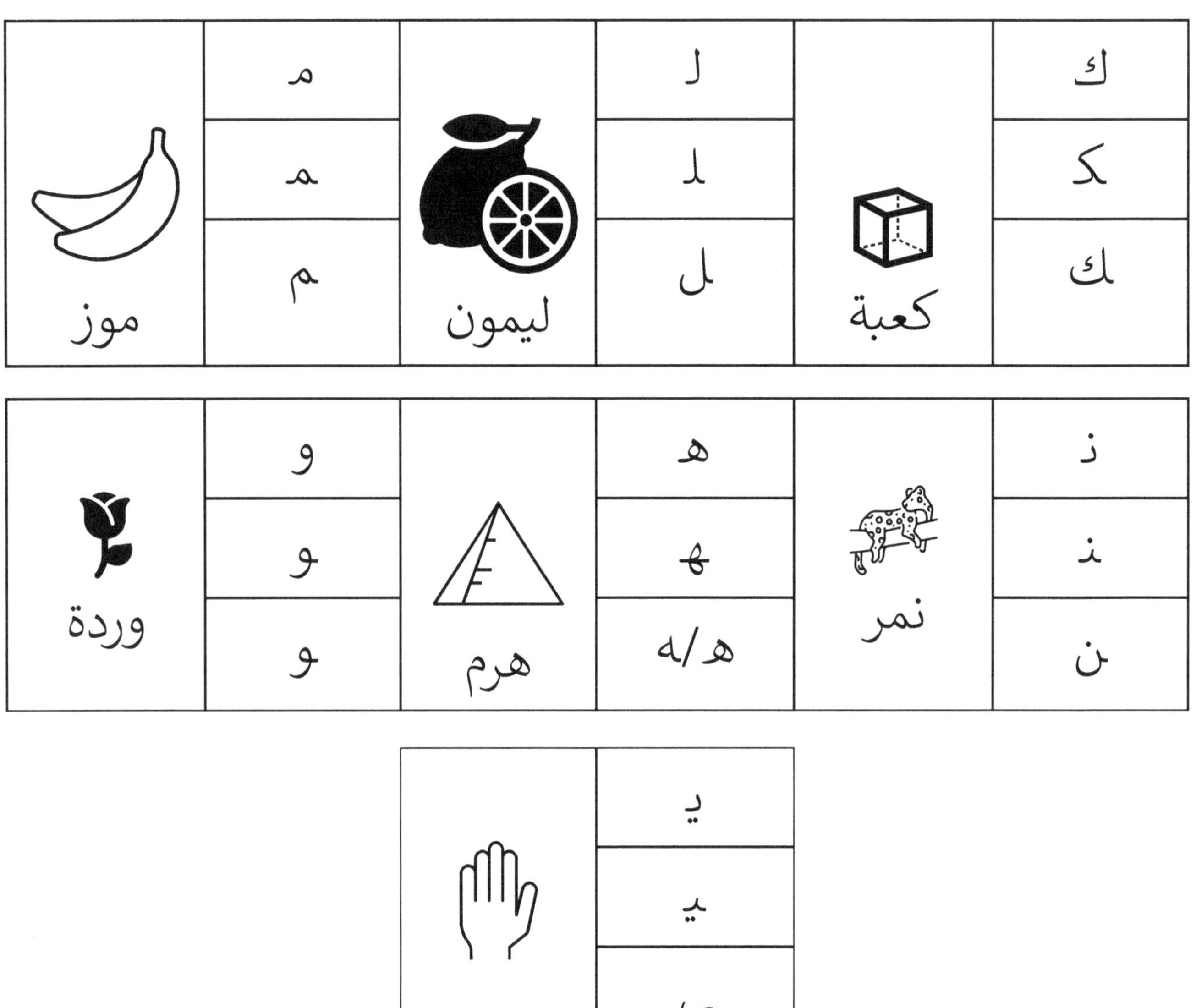

Info box:

You will notice on page five that some letters have a either a line above or below them e.g.

bā, ṣād, nūn

This is because Arabic has some sounds and letters that are different to English. You will notice these differences once you listen to the audio for the alphabet.

الأبجدية العربية

> **In this unit you will learn to:**
>
> ✓ Spell your name in Arabic
> ✓ Recognise and identify the letters of the alphabet
> ✓ Read the different vowels in Arabic

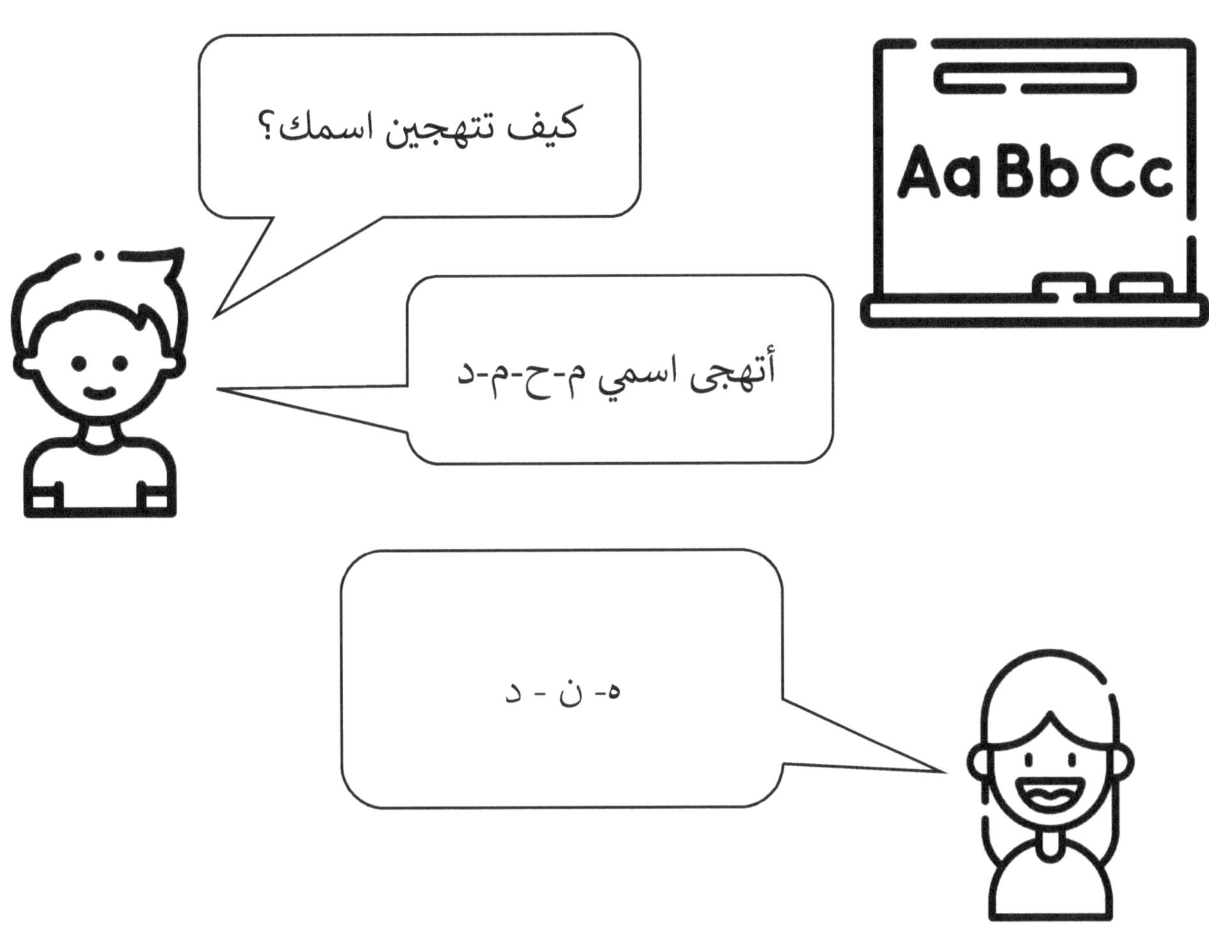

I can hear and pronounce Arabic letters

The letters of the Arabic alphabet 

ج jīm	ث thā	ت tā	ب bā	ا alif
ر rā	ذ dhāl	د dāl	خ khā	ح hā
ض dād	ص sād	ش shīn	س sīn	ز zāy
ف fā	غ ghayn	ع 'ayn	ظ zhā	ط tā
ن nūn	م mīm	ل lām	ك kāf	ق qāf
	ي yā	ء hamzah	و wāw	ه hā

The different shapes for the letters

د د dāl	خ خ خ خ khā	ح ح ح ح hā	ج ج ج ج jīm	ث ث ث ث thā	ت تـتـت tā	ب بـبـب bā	ا ا alif
ط ط ط ط ط tā	ض ضـضـض ض dād	ص صـصـص ص sād	ش شـشـش ش shīn	س سـسـس س sīn	زز zāy	رـر rā	ذ ذ dhāl
م مـمـم mīm	ل لـلـل lām	ك كـكـك kāf	ق قـقـق qāf	ف فـف ف fā	غـغـغـغ ghayn	عـعـعـع 'ayn	ظ ظـظـظ ظ zhā
		ي يـيـي yā	أ ؤئـئـء hamzah	وـو wāw	هـهـهـه hā	ن نـنـن nūn	

THE LANGUAGE GYM

1. Match the Arabic letter with the English sound

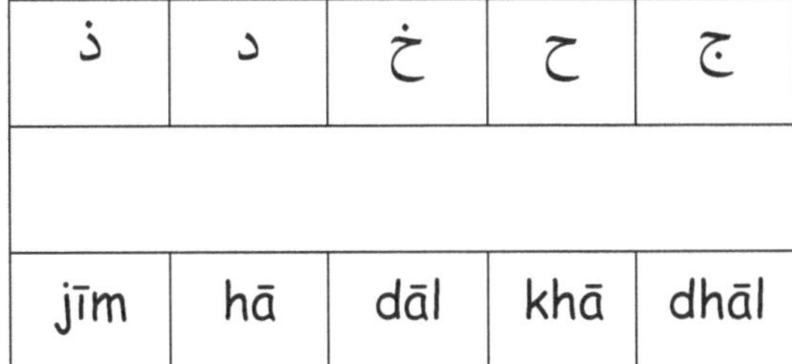

ذ	د	خ	ح	ج
jīm	hā	dāl	khā	dhāl

ت	ب	ث	ا
thā	alif	tā	bā

2. Add dots to the letters where they are needed

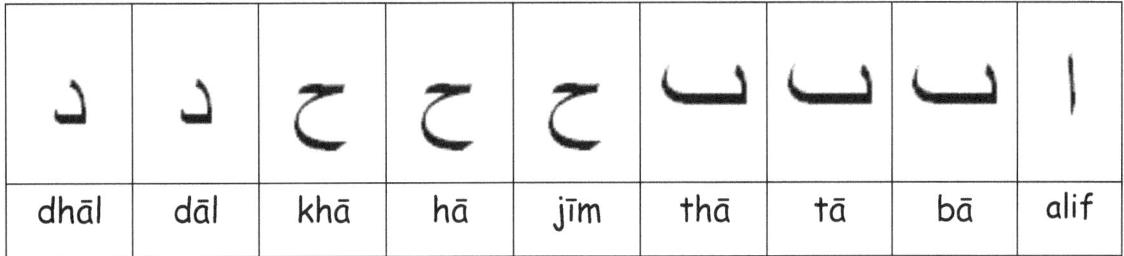

د	د	ح	ح	ح	ب	ب	ب	ا
dhāl	dāl	khā	hā	jīm	thā	tā	bā	alif

3. Trace and then copy the letters

trace letter ➡ ا ب ت ث ج ح خ د ذ

copy letter ➡

4. Listen and circle the correct letter

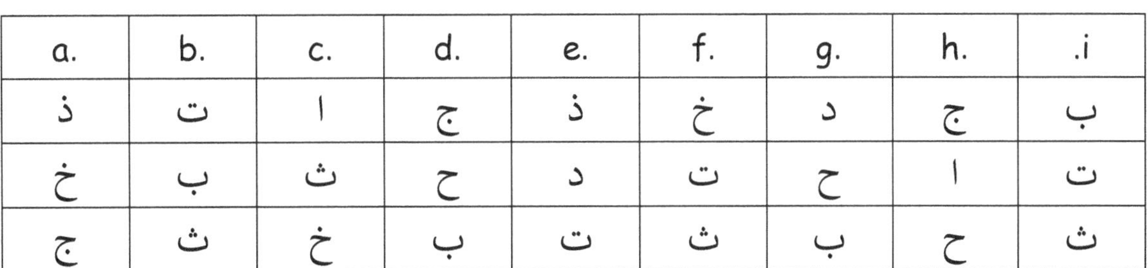

a.	b.	c.	d.	e.	f.	g.	h.	.i
ذ	ت	ا	ج	ذ	خ	د	ج	ب
خ	ب	ث	ح	د	ت	ح	ا	ت
ج	ث	خ	ب	ت	ث	ب	ح	ث

THE LANGUAGE GYM

5. Match the Arabic letter with the English sound

ع	ظ	غ	ض	ط	ص
ghayn	'ayn	<u>zh</u>ā	<u>t</u>ā	<u>d</u>ād	<u>s</u>ād

ر	ز	ش	س
shīn	sīn	zāy	rā

6. Add dots to the letters where they are needed

ع	ع	ط	ط	ص	ص	س	س	ر	ر
ghayn	'ayn	<u>zh</u>ā	<u>t</u>ā	<u>d</u>ād	<u>s</u>ād	shīn	sīn	zāy	rā

7. Trace and then copy the letters

trace letter ➡ 

copy letter ➡

8. Listen and circle the correct letter

a.	b.	c.	d.	e.	f.	g.	h.	i.	j.
ا	س	ط	ج	ظ	ض	س	د	ص	ر
ع	ص	ب	غ	ح	د	ت	ز	ا	س
ح	ج	ت	خ	ب	ب	ع	ت	ش	ز

THE LANGUAGE GYM

9. Match the Arabic letter with the English sound

هـ	م	ي	ء	ن	و
hamza	yā	hā	wāw	nūn	mīm

ق	ف	ل	ك
lām	kāf	qāf	fā

10. Add dots to the letters where they are needed

ى	و	هـ	ں	م	ل	ڡ	ڡ
yā	wāw	hā	nūn	mīm	lām	qāf	fā

11. Trace and then copy the letters

trace letter ➡

copy letter ➡

12. Listen and circle the correct letter

a.	b.	c.	d.	e.	f.	g.	h.	i.	j.
ل	ي	ء	ك	هـ	ف	ر	م	ن	ق
م	ب	ت	م	ح	ث	و	ب	ت	ك
ا	ج	ث	ق	ي	ت	ذ	ل	ث	ف

THE LANGUAGE GYM

Unit 1.2 Letters in various forms

Info box: letters come in various shapes

ending	middle	beginning		
ا	ا	ا	⇐	ا alif
ب	ـبـ	بـ	⇐	ب bā
ت	ـتـ	تـ	⇐	ت tā
ث	ـثـ	ثـ	⇐	ث thā

1. Trace and copy out the letters

ending	middle	beginning		
ا	ا	ا	trace	ا
			copy	
ب	ـبـ	بـ	trace	ب
			copy	
ت	ـتـ	تـ	trace	ت
			copy	
ث	ـثـ	ثـ	trace	ث
			copy	

2. Circle which form the following are:

beginning (b) , middle (m), end (e) or the whole (w)

٦. ـت   ٥. ڎ   ٤. ا   ٣. ثـ   ٢. ـبـ   ١. ت

e w b   b e m   e b w   m w e   m e b   e m b

3. Draw a line from the beginning of the letter to the middle and then end

ثـ	ـتـ	ثُ	ا
ـب	بـ	ا	ب
ـت	ا	بـ	ت
ا	ثـ	ـت	ث

4. Fill in the gap with the correct form of the missing letter

ending	middle	beginning	
أنـ	ثمــني	ـسمي	ا
كـ	ســع	ـلال	ب
ـس	اثنــا	ـسع	ت
ثلا	تــلج	ـلاث	ث

THE LANGUAGE GYM

Info box: letters come in various shapes

ending	middle	beginning		
جـ	ـجـ	جـ	⇦	ج jīm
حـ	ـحـ	حـ	⇦	ح hā
خـ	ـخـ	خـ	⇦	خ khā
ـد	ـد	د	⇦	د dāl
ـذ	ـذ	ذ	⇦	ذ dhāl

5. Trace and copy out the letters

ending	middle	beginning		
جـ	ـجـ	جـ	trace	ج
			copy	
حـ	ـحـ	حـ	trace	ح
			copy	
خـ	ـخـ	خـ	trace	خ
			copy	
ـد	ـد	د	trace	د
			copy	
ـذ	ـذ	ذ	trace	ذ
			copy	

6. Circle which form the following are:

beginning (b) , middle (m), end (e) or the whole (w)

٦. جـ	٥. د	٤. خـ	٣. ـذ	٢. ـحـ	١. ـج
m w b	b e m	e b w	m w e	m e b	e m b

THE LANGUAGE GYM

7. Draw a line from the beginning of the letter to the middle and then end

ـد	خـ	ذ	ج
خ	ـد	جـ	ح
ح	ـحـ	د	خ
ج	ـذ	خـ	د
ـذ	جـ	ـحـ	ذ

8. Fill in the gap with the correct form of the missing letter

ending	middle	beginning	
تثل__	الـ__و	__ميل	ج
مل__	الـ__ادي	__سن	ح
مطب__	الـ__امس	__مس	خ
خال__	لـ__ي	__جاجة	د
تلمي__	لـ__يذ	__بابة	ذ

THE LANGUAGE GYM

Info box: letters come in various shapes

ending	middle	beginning		
ر	ـر	ر	⇐	ر rā
ز	ـز	ز	⇐	ز zāy
س	ـسـ	سـ	⇐	س sīn
ش	ـشـ	شـ	⇐	ش shīn
ص	ـصـ	صـ	⇐	ص <u>s</u>ād
ض	ـضـ	ضـ	⇐	ض <u>d</u>ād

9. Trace and copy out the letters

ending	middle	beginning		
ر ز	ر ز	رز	trace	راز
			copy	
ـس	ـسـ	سـ	trace	س
			copy	
ـش	ـشـ	شـ	trace	ش
			copy	
ـص	ـصـ	صـ	trace	ص
			copy	
ـض	ـضـ	ضـ	trace	ض
			copy	

10. Circle which form the following are:

beginning (b) , middle (m), end (e) or the whole (w)

١. ص   ٢. ضـ   ٣. ر   ٤. ـشـ   ٥. ـس   ٦. ص

m w b   b e m   e m w   m w e   m e b   e m b

THE LANGUAGE GYM

11. Draw a line from the beginning of the letter to the middle and then end

رـز	ضـ	س	رز
ض	رـز	ش	س
ص	صـ	رز	ش
ش	ـسـ	ضـ	ص
س	شـ	صـ	ض

12. Fill in the gap with the correct form of the missing letter

ending	middle	beginning	
الخيـــ	عمـــي	ـــمادي	ر
مركـــ	يـــيد	ـــار	ز
ملابـــ	تـــع	ـــبع	س
مشمـــ	مـــمس	ـــمس	ش
مقـــ	بـــل	ـــباح	ص
أبيـــ	مـــغوط	ـــرس	ض

THE LANGUAGE GYM

Info box: letters come in various shapes

ending	middle	beginning		
ظ ط	ظ ط	ظ ط	⇐	zhā ṭā ط ظ
ع خ	ـعـ ـغـ	ـع ـغ	⇐	ghayn ayn ع غ
ف	ـفـ	ف	⇐	fā ف
ق	ـقـ	ق	⇐	qāf ق
ك	ـك	ک	⇐	kāf ك

13. Trace and copy out the letters

ending	middle	beginning		
ظ ط	ظ ط	ظ ط	trace	ط \ ظ
			copy	
خ ع	ـخـ ـعـ	ـغ ـع	trace	ع \ غ
			copy	
ـف	ـفـ	ف	trace	ف
			copy	
ـق	ـقـ	ق	trace	ق
			copy	
ـك	ـك	ک	trace	ك
			copy	

14. Circle which form the following are:

beginning (b) , middle (m), end (e) or the whole (w)

٦. ط	٥. ق	٤. ع	٣. غ	٢. ف	١. ك
m w b	b e m	e b w	m w e	m e b	e m b

THE LANGUAGE GYM

15. Draw a line from the beginning of the letter to the middle and then end

ع خ	ط ظ	ف	غ ع
ط ظ	ـعـغ	ك	ط ظ
ق	ـق	ع غ	ف
ك	ـف	ط ظ	ق
ف	ـك	ق	ك

16. Fill in the gap with the correct form of the missing letter

ending	middle	beginning	
تسـ__	الـ__اشر	__مري	ع
مضغو__	مسـ__رة	__ائر	ط
__مل	مـ__كرة	__براير	ف
بطريـ__	مـ__لمة	__مر	ق
__مل	سـ__ر	__تاب	ك

Info box: letters come in various shapes

ending	middle	beginning		
ل	ـلـ	لـ	⇐	ل lām
ـم	ـمـ	مـ	⇐	م mīm
ـن	ـنـ	نـ	⇐	ن nūn
ـه	ـهـ	هـ	⇐	ه hā
ـو	ـو	و	⇐	و wāw
ـي	ـيـ	يـ	⇐	ي yā

17. Trace and copy out the letters

ending	middle	beginning		
ل	ـلـ	لـ	trace	ل
			copy	
ـم	ـمـ	مـ	trace	م
			copy	
ـن	ـنـ	نـ	trace	ن
			copy	
ـه	ـهـ	هـ	trace	ه
			copy	
ـو	ـو	و	trace	و
			copy	
ـي	ـيـ	يـ	trace	ي
			copy	

18. Draw a line from the beginning of the letter to the middle and then end

مـ	لـ	هـ	ل
ل	ـمـ	و	م
ن	ـيـ	ي	ن
ي	و	ل	ه
و	ـهـ	ذ	و
ه	ـنـ	مـ	ي

19. Fill in the gap with the correct form of the missing letter

ending	middle	beginning	
ليـ__	مـ__ف	__يل	ل
قل__	مقلـ__ة	__فكرة	م
الثامـ__	حسـ__ى	__مر	ن
إنـ__	مـ__ندس	__ند	ه
قال__ا	لـ__ن	__احد	و
__سمـ	لـ__لة	__وسف	ي

THE LANGUAGE GYM

20. Write the underlined letter in its whole form

ة	<u>ن</u>	س	=	سنة
ع	س		=	تِسع
ر		ع	=	عشِر
ع		س	=	سبع
ف		م	=	ملِف
ب	ل		=	كِلب
ة	ط		=	قِطة
ب		ب	=	باب

21. Write the words correctly using the given letters

كتب	=	ب	ت	ك
	=	أ	ر	ق
	=	ح	ت	ف
	=	ر	ص	ن
	=	ب	ه	ذ
	=	ر	ب	ص
	=	ج	ر	خ
	=	ل	خ	د

UNIT 1 – ANSWERS - ALPHABET

1. **Match the Arabic letter with the English sound**

   alif ا   bā ب   tā ت   thā ث   jīm ج   hā ح   khā خ   dāl د   dhāl ذ

2. **Add dots to the letters where they are needed**

ذ	د	خ	ح	ج	ث	ت	ب	ا
dhāl	dāl	khā	hā	jīm	thā	tā	bā	alif

3. **Trace and copy the letter**

   Ensure the shapes of the letters are correctly traced and copied.

4. **Listen and circle the correct letter**

   ج .*a*   ب .*b*   ث .*c*   ح .*d*   ذ .*e*   خ .*f*   د .*g*   ا .*h*   ت .*i*

5. **Match the Arabic letter with the English sound**

   rā ر   zā ز   sīn س   shīn ش   sād ص   dād ض   tā ط   zhā ظ   'ayn ع   ghayn غ

6. **Add dots to the letters where they are needed**

غ	ع	ظ	ط	ض	ص	ش	س	ز	ر
ghayn	'ayn	<u>zh</u>ā	<u>t</u>ā	<u>d</u>ād	<u>s</u>ād	shīn	sīn	zā	rā

7. **Trace and copy the letter**

   Ensure the shapes of the letters are correctly traced and copied.

8. **Listen and circle the correct letter**

   ع .*a*   ص .*b*   ط .*c*   غ .*d*   ظ .*e*   ض .*f*   س .*g*   ز .*h*   ش .*i*   ر .*j*

9. **Match the Arabic letter with the English sound**

   fā ف   qāf ق   kāf ك   lām ل   mīm م   nūn ن   wāw و   hā ه   yā ي   hamza ء

10. **Add dots to the letters where they are needed**

ي	و	ه	ن	م	ل	ق	ف
yā	wāw	hā	nūn	mīm	lām	qāf	fā

11. **Trace and copy the letter**

   Ensure the shapes of the letters are correctly traced and copied.

12. **Listen and circle the correct letter**

   ل .*a*   ي .*b*   ء .*c*   ك .*d*   ه .*e*   ف .*f*   و .*g*   م .*h*   ن .*i*   ق .*j*

Unit 1.2 Letters in various forms

1. Trace and copy the letter

Ensure the shapes of the letters are correctly traced and copied.

2. Circle which form the following are:

٦. ت	٥. ڎ	٤. ا	٣. ـث	٢. ـبـ	١. ت
e	b	e	e	m	b

3. Draw a line from the beginning of the letter to the middle and then end

ـا	ـا	ا	ا
ـبـ	ـبـ	بـ	ب
ـتـ	ـتـ	تـ	ت
ـثـ	ـثـ	ثـ	ث

4. Fill in the gap with the correct form of the missing letter

ending	middle	beginning	
أنا	ثماني	اسمي	ا
كلب	سبع	بلال	ب
ست	اثنتا	تسع	ت
ثلاث	تثلج	ثلاث	ث

5. Trace and copy the letter

Ensure the shapes of the letters are correctly traced and copied.

6. Circle whether the following is beginning, middle or end

٦. جـ	٥. د	٤. ـخ	٣. ـذ	٢. ـحـ	١. جـ
m	b	e	e	m	b

THE LANGUAGE GYM

7. **Draw a line from the beginning of the letter to the middle and then end**

ج		ﺟ		ﺟ		ج
ح		ﺤ		ﺤ		ح
خ		ﺨ		ﺨ		خ
ﺪ		ﺪ		ﺩ		د
ﺬ		ﺬ		ﺫ		ذ

8. **Fill in the gap with the correct form of the missing letter**

ending	middle	beginning	
تثلج	الجو	جميل	ج
ملح	الحادي	حسن	ح
مطبخ	الخامس	خمس	خ
خالد	لدي	دجاجة	د
تلميذ	لذيذ	ذبابة	ذ

9. **Trace and copy the letter**

Ensure the shapes of the letters are correctly traced and copied.

10. **Circle which form the following are:**

٦. ص   ٥. س   ٤. ش   ٣. ر   ٢. ض   ١. ص

w   b   m   w   m   e

THE LANGUAGE GYM

11. **Draw a line from the beginning of the letter to the middle and then end**

رـز		رـز		رز		رز
س		ســ		ـس		س
ش		شـ		ـشـ		ش
ص		صـ		ـصـ		ص
ض		ضـ		ـضـ		ض

12. **Fill in the gap with the correct form of the missing letter**

ending	middle	beginning	
الخير	عمري	رمادي	ر
مركز	يزيد	زار	ز
ملابس	تسع	سبع	س
مشمس	مشمس	شمس	ش
مقق	بصل	صباح	ص
أبيض	مضغوط	ضرس	ض

13. **Trace and copy the letter**

Ensure the shapes of the letters are correctly traced and copied.

14. **Circle which form the following are:**

٦. ط	٥. ق	٤. ع	٣. غـ	٢. فـ	١. كـ
w	b	e	m	m	b

THE LANGUAGE GYM

15. Draw a line from the beginning of the letter to the middle and then end

ع غ		ـع ـغ		ء غ		ع غ
ط ظ		ط ظ		ط ظ		ط ظ
ف		ـف		ف		ف
ق		ـق		ق		ق
ك		ك		ك		ك

16. Fill in the gap with the correct form of the missing letter

ending	middle	beginning	
تسع	العاشر	عمري	ع
مضغوط	مسطرة	طائر	ط
ملف	مفكرة	فبراير	ف
بطريق	مقلمة	قمر	ق
ملك	سكر	كتاب	ك

17. Trace and copy the letter

Ensure the shapes of the letters are correctly traced and copied.

18. Draw a line from the beginning of the letter to the middle and then end

لـ		ـلـ		ـل		ل
مـ		ـمـ		ـم		م
نـ		ـنـ		ـن		ن
هـ		ـهـ		ـه		ه
و		و		و		و
يـ		ـيـ		ـي		ي

19. Fill in the gap with the correct form of the missing letter

ending	middle	beginning	
ليل	ملف	ليل	ل
قلم	مقلمة	مفكرة	م
الثامن	حسنى	نمر	ن
إنه	مهندس	هند	ه
قالوا	لون	واحد	و
اسمي	ليلة	يوسف	ي

20. Write the underlined letter in it's whole form

ة	ن	س	=	سنة
ع	س	ت	=	تسع
ر	ش	ع	=	عشر
ع	ب	س	=	سبع
ف	ل	م	=	ملف
ب	ل	ك	=	كلب
ة	ط	ق	=	قطة
ب	ا	ب	=	باب

21. Write the words correctly using the given letters

كَتَبَ	=	ب	ت	ك
قرأ	=	أ	ر	ق
فتح	=	ح	ت	ف
نصر	=	ر	ص	ن
ذهب	=	ب	ه	ذ
صبر	=	ر	ب	ص
خرج	=	ج	ر	خ
دخل	=	ل	خ	د

UNIT 2

الحركات

In this unit you will learn to:

- ✓ Read the different vowels in Arabic

THE LANGUAGE GYM

UNIT 2. VOWELS
I can hear and pronounce the vowels in Arabic

Info box: Arabic has a variety of vowels that impact the sound of the letter. Listen and repeat.

Fatha - ◌َ - 'a' sound and always comes above the letter

رَ	ذَ	دَ	خَ	حَ	جَ	ثَ	تَ	بَ	اَ
ra	tha	da	kha	ha	ja	tha	ta	ba	a
فَ	غَ	عَ	ظَ	طَ	ضَ	صَ	شَ	سَ	زَ
fa	gha	'a	tha	ta	dha	sa	sha	sa	za
	يَ	وَ	هَ	نَ	مَ	لَ	كَ	قَ	
	ya	wa	ha	na	ma	la	ka	qa	

Kasra - ◌ِ - 'i' sound and always comes below the letter

رِ	ذِ	دِ	خِ	حِ	جِ	ثِ	تِ	بِ	اِ
ri	thi	di	khi	hi	ji	thi	ti	bi	i
فِ	غِ	عِ	ظِ	طِ	ضِ	صِ	شِ	سِ	زِ
fi	ghi	'i	thi	ti	dhi	si	shi	si	zi
	يِ	وِ	هِ	نِ	مِ	لِ	كِ	قِ	
	yi	wi	hi	ni	mi	li	ki	qi	

Dhamma - ◌ُ - 'u' sound and always comes above the letter

رُ	ذُ	دُ	خُ	حُ	جُ	ثُ	تُ	بُ	اُ
ru	thu	du	khu	hu	ju	thu	tu	bu	u
فُ	غُ	عُ	ظُ	طُ	ضُ	صُ	شُ	سُ	زُ
fu	ghu	'u	thu	tu	dhu	su	shu	su	zu
	يُ	وُ	هُ	نُ	مُ	لُ	كُ	قُ	
	yu	wu	hu	nu	mu	lu	ku	qu	

2.1 - Fatha

A. أ-ذ – Listen, read alour then copy the words underneath with fatha 🔊

قَرَأَ	سَأَلَ	أَخَذَ	أَ
……………	……………	……………	
كَتَبَ	عَبَدَ	بَدَأَ	بَ
……………	……………	……………	
نَبَتَ	فَتَحَ	تَجَرَ	تَ
……………	……………	……………	
بَحَثَ	مَثَلَ	ثَبَتَ	ثَ
……………	……………	……………	
خَرَجَ	سَجَدَ	جَلَسَ	جَ
……………	……………	……………	
جَرَحَ	نَحَرَ	حَصَدَ	حَ
……………	……………	……………	
طَبَخَ	أَخَذَ	خَلَعَ	خَ
……………	……………	……………	
فَسَدَ	صَدَمَ	دَخَلَ	دَ
……………	……………	……………	
نَبَذَ	نَذَرَ	ذَكَرَ	ذَ
……………	……………	……………	

THE LANGUAGE GYM

صَبَرَ	تَرَكَ	رَكَّلَ	رَ
....	....	....	
لَمَزَ	هَزَمَ	زَرَعَ	زَ
....	....	....	
حَبَسَ	وَسَطَ	سَتَرَ	سَ
....	....	....	
فَرَشَ	كَشَفَ	شَكَرَ	شَ
....	....	....	
نَكَصَ	نَصَحَ	صَرَعَ	صَ
....	....	....	
رَفَضَ	حَضَرَ	ضَرَبَ	ضَ
....	....	....	
رَبَطَ	خَطَرَ	طَلَبَ	طَ
....	....	....	
وَعَظَ	نَظَرَ	ظَلَمَ	ظَ
....	....	....	
دَفَعَ	فَعَلَ	عَقَدَ	عَ
....	....	....	
بَلَغَ	شَغَلَ	غَسَلَ	غَ
....	....	....	

C. ف-ي – Listen, read along then copy the words underneath

وَقَفَ	نَفَعَ	فَقَدَ	فَ
....	....	....	
خَلَقَ	سَقَطَ	قَرَعَ	قَ
....	....	....	
مَسَكَ	سَكَبَ	كَذَبَ	كَ
....	....	....	
فَصَلَ	قَلَبَ	لَمَسَ	لَ
....	....	....	
حَكَمَ	هَمَزَ	مَسَحَ	مَ
....	....	....	
وَزَنَ	مَنَعَ	نَصَحَ	نَ
....	....	....	
أَلَهَ	ظَهَرَ	هَمَزَ	هَ
....	....	....	
فَسَدَ	عَوَرَ	وَجَدَ	وَ
....	....	....	
		يَنَعَ	يَ
		....	

The underlined letters indicate common mispronunciations

نَظَرَ	نَذَرَ	رَضَعَ	رَدَعَ	بَطَرَ	بَتَرَ
خَتَرَ	خَطَرَ	رَكَدَ	رَكَضَ	حَسَدَ	حَصَدَ
وَكَزَ	وَقَرَ	غَفَرَ	فَرَغَ	قَصَمَ	قَسَمَ
كَسَفَ	قَصَفَ	رَقَدَ	رَكَدَ	سَكَتَ	سَقَطَ
مَرَضَ	مَرَدَ	قَنَطَ	قَنَتَ	حَظَرَ	حَذَرَ
هَمَزَ	هَمَسَ	فَرَدَ	فَرَضَ	رَسَمَ	رَصَفَ
بَرَكَ	مَكَرَ	خَطَبَ	خَتَمَ	مَسَحَ	سَمَحَ
حَرَسَ	حَرَثَ	بَطَلَ	طَلَبَ	خَصَفَ	خَسَفَ

THE LANGUAGE GYM

خَلَقَ وَرَزَقَ	دَخَلَ وَخَرَجَ	طَلَعَ وَنَزَلَ
....	....	....
فَهَرَ وَقَمَعَ	رَبَطَ يَدَكَ	قَلَبَ وَعَكَسَ
....	....	....
زَرَعَ وَحَصَدَ	سَئَلَ فَعَرَفَ	حَلَفَ فَصَدَقَ
....	....	....
عَبَدَ وَشَكَرَ	هَبَطَ فَسَجَدَ	رَكَعَ فَرَفَعَ
....	....	....

غَدَرَ وَكَذَبَ فَقَتَلَ	مَلَكَ وَحَكَمَ فَعَدَلَ
....	....
طَحَنَ وَخَبَزَ فَأَكَلَ	سَتَرَ وَغَفَرَ فَعَتَقَ
....	....
بَلَغَ فَعَقَلَ وَرَشَدَ	قَرَأَ وَكَتَبَ فَنَجَحَ
....	....

			.١ wāhid
....	....	....	.٢ ithnān
....	....	....	.٣ thalātha
....	....	....	.٤ arb'a
....	....	....	.٥ khamsa
....	....	....	.٦ sitta
....	....	....	.٧ sab'a
....	....	....	.٨ thamāniya
....			.٩ tis'a
....			.١٠ 'ashara

THE LANGUAGE GYM

2.2 - Kasra

Kasra - ِ - 'i' sound and always comes below the letter									
رِ	ذِ	دِ	خِ	حِ	جِ	ثِ	تِ	بِ	اِ
ri	thi	di	khi	hi	ji	thi	ti	bi	i
فِ	غِ	عِ	ظِ	طِ	ضِ	صِ	شِ	سِ	زِ
fi	ghi	'i	thi	ti	dhi	si	shi	si	zi
		يِ	وِ	هِ	نِ	مِ	لِ	كِ	قِ
		yi	wi	hi	ni	mi	li	ki	qi

Practise reading the following letters and words with fatha and kasra.

جَجِ	ثَثِ	تَتِ	بَبِ	أَإِ
رَرِ	ذَذِ	دَدِ	خَخِ	حَحِ
ضَضِ	صَصِ	شَشِ	سَسِ	زَزِ
فَفِ	غَغِ	عَعِ	ظَظِ	طَطِ
نَنِ	مَمِ	لَلِ	كَكِ	قَقِ
تَةِ	يَيِ	ءَءِ	وَوِ	هَهِ

A. Listen, read along and then copy the words underneath with fatha and kasra. ((◼

عَجِبَ	خَجِلَ	وَتَرَ	شَبِعَ	رَبِحَ	إِرَمَ	١. wāhid
حَزِنَ	فَرِحَ	أَذِنَ	نَدِمَ	بَخِلَ	رَحِمَ	٢. ithnān
عَطِشَ	رَضِيَ	لَصِقَ	خَشِيَ	نَشِطَ	نَسِيَ	٣. thalātha
رَكِبَ	بَقِيَ	حَفِظَ	رَغِبَ	لَعِبَ	حَظِيَ	٤. arb'a
دَهِشَ	قَوِيَ	فَهِمَ	غَنِمَ	عَمِلَ	عَلِمَ	٥. khamsa
عَمَلِه	سَخِرَ	غَلَسِ	بَدَتِ	تَعِبَ	صَعِدَ	٦. sitta

وَلَدِكَ	بِقَلَمٍ	وَهِيَ	سَمِعَ	سَبَبٍ	سَهِرَ	١. wāhid
بِثَمَرِهِ	عِصَمٍ	جِهَةً	سِمَةً	يَدَهِ	نَشِطَ	٢. ithnān
لِوَلَدِكَ	بَلَدٍ	وَصَلَتِ	وَرَقٍ	عَمَلٍ	غَضِبَ	٣. thalātha
أَكَلَ فَشَبِعَ وَعَطِشَ فَشَرِبَ						٤. arb'a

2. Listen and then write the following words with fathah and kasra.

			١. wāhid
			٢. ithnān
			٣. thalātha
			٤. arb'a

THE LANGUAGE GYM

2.3 - Dhamma

				Dhamma - ُ◌ - 'u' sound and always comes above the letter					
رُ	ذُ	دُ	خُ	حُ	جُ	ثُ	تُ	بُ	اُ
ru	thu	du	khu	hu	ju	thu	tu	bu	u
فُ	غُ	عُ	ظُ	طُ	ضُ	صُ	شُ	سُ	زُ
fu	ghu	'u	thu	tu	dhu	su	shu	su	zu
		يُ	وُ	هُ	نُ	مُ	لُ	كُ	قُ
		yu	wu	hu	nu	mu	lu	ku	qu

جَجِجُ	ثَثِثُ	تَتِتُ	بَبِبُ	اَإِأُ
رَرِرُ	ذَذِذُ	دَدِدُ	خَخِخُ	حَحِحُ
ضَضِضُ	صَصِصُ	شَشِشُ	سَسِسُ	زَزِزُ
فَفِفُ	غَغِغُ	عَعِعُ	ظَظِظُ	طَطِطُ
نَنِنُ	مَمِمُ	لَلِلُ	كَكِكُ	قَقِقُ
تَّةُ	يَيِيُ	ءَءِءُ	وَوِوُ	هَهِهُ

A. Listen, read along then copy the following: 🔊

#						
١. wāhid	أُسِرَ	بُعِثَ	تُلِيَ	ثُقِب	جُرِعَ	حُمِلَ
٢. ithnān	خُلِقَ	دُرِسَ	ذُبِحَ	رُزِقَ	زُرِعَ	سُرِقَ
٣. thalātha	شُرِحَ	صُعِقَ	ضُرِب	طُلِب	ظُلِمَ	عُتِقَ
٤. arb'a	غُسِلَ	فُتِحَ	قُتِلَ	كُسِرَ	لُعِنَ	مُنِعَ
٥. khamsa	وُلِدَ	هُدِيَ	سُئِلَ	قُطِعَ	مُنِعَ	رُسُلُ
٦. sitta	لَطُفَ	كَبُرَ	صَغُرَ	عَظُمَ	رَخُصَ	كَثُرَ
٧. sab'a	قَرُبَ	بَعُدَ	سَهُلَ	صَعُبَ	ثَقُلَ	تَصِلُ
٨. thamāniya	يَرِثُ	يَعِظُ	يَقَعُ	تَقِفُ	تَضَعُ	حَسُنَ

THE LANGUAGE GYM

١. *wāhid*	أَجْعَلَ	لَلَبِثَ	لَأَجِدُ	لِأَهَبَ	لِأَجَلِ	لِرَجُلِ
٢. *ithnān*	وَحُذِفَ	فَجُمِعَ	وَدُبِغَ	فَضُرِبَ	فَطُبِعَ	نَسِمُهُ
٣. *thalātha*	لَكُمْ	يَعِظُهُ	جُمَعِهِ	مَعَهُمْ	لَعَلِمَهُ	أَحَدَكُمْ
٤. *arb'a*	وَثُلْثَهُ	خُمُسَهُ	نَبَؤُهُ	سَنَسِمُهُ	فَجَعَلَهُ	يَعِظُكُمْ
٥. *khamsa*	حَسُنَ خَلْقُهُ وَكَمُلَ أَدَبُهُ			قُرِئَ وَرَقُكَ وَكُتِبَ بِقَلَمِكَ
٦. *sitta*	وَقَفَ حَسَنُ يَعِظُ وَلَدَهُ، فَحَضَرَ عُمَرُ وَوَقَفَ مَعَهُ
٧. *sab'a*	فَتَحَ كَرَمُ كُتُبَهُ وَقَرَأَ،فَسَمِعَهُ عُمَرُ وَقَرَأَ مَعَهُ

THE LANGUAGE GYM

....	....	....	١. wāhid
....	....	....	٢. ithnān
....	....	....	٣. thalātha
....	....	....	٤. arb'a
....	....	....	٥. khamsa
....	....	....	٦. sitta
....	....	....	٧. sab'a
....	....	....	٨. thamāniya
....			٩. tis'a
....			١٠. 'ashara

UNIT 2 - ANSWERS – Al Harakaat – The 'a' 'i' 'u' Vowels

1. Listen and then write the following words with fathah

مَكَرَ	خَتَمَ	أَخَذَ	.١ wāhid
فَتَحَ	بَدَأَ	سَبَحَ	.٢ ithnān
نَصَرَ	كَتَبَ	قَرَأَ	.٣ thalātha
مَرَضَ	بَرَكَ	نَجَحَ	.٤ arb'a
كَسَفَ	حَظَرَ	حَسَدَ	.٥ khamsa
سَئَلَ	طَلَبَ	نَظَرَ	.٦ sitta
فَرَدَ	خَسَفَ	ضَرَبَ	.٧ sab'a
رَصَفَ	سَكَتَ	هَمَسَ	.٨ thamāniya
مَلَكَ وَحَكَمَ فَعَدَلَ			.٩ tis'a
بَلَغَ فَعَقَلَ وَرَشَدَ			.١٠ 'ashara

2. Listen and then write the following words with fathah and kasrah

سَمِعَ	بِقَلَمِهِ	وَلَدِهِ	.١ wāhid
عَطِشَ	حَمِدَ	رَكِبَ	.٢ ithnān
حَسِبَ	وَرَقِة	غَضِبَ	.٣ thalātha
كَتَبَ مَعَ قَلَمِهِ			.٤ arb'a

THE LANGUAGE GYM

3. Listen and then write the following words with fathah, kasrah and dhammah.

فُتِحَ	غُسِلَ	كُتِبَ	.١ wāhid
رُكِبَ	جُلِسَ	ضُرِبَ	.٢ ithnān
وُلِدَ	يَعِظُ	تَضَعُ	.٣ thalātha
قُرِئَ	فَفُتِحُ	أَجَعَلَ	.٤ arb'a
تَصِلَ	كُرِبَ	لَلَبِثُ	.٥ khamsa
دُرِسَ	هُدِيَ	رُسُلُ	.٦ sitta
جُرِعَ	حُمِلَ	كَثُرَ	.٧ sab'a
فَجَعَلَهُ	وَثُلُثَهُ	مَعَهُمُ	.٨ thamāniya
	قُرِئَ وَرَقُكَ		.٩ tis'a
	وَكَتَبَ بِقَلَمِكَ		.١٠ 'ashara

THE LANGUAGE GYM

UNIT 3

السكون

In this unit you will learn to:

✓ Identify and read words with a sukoon

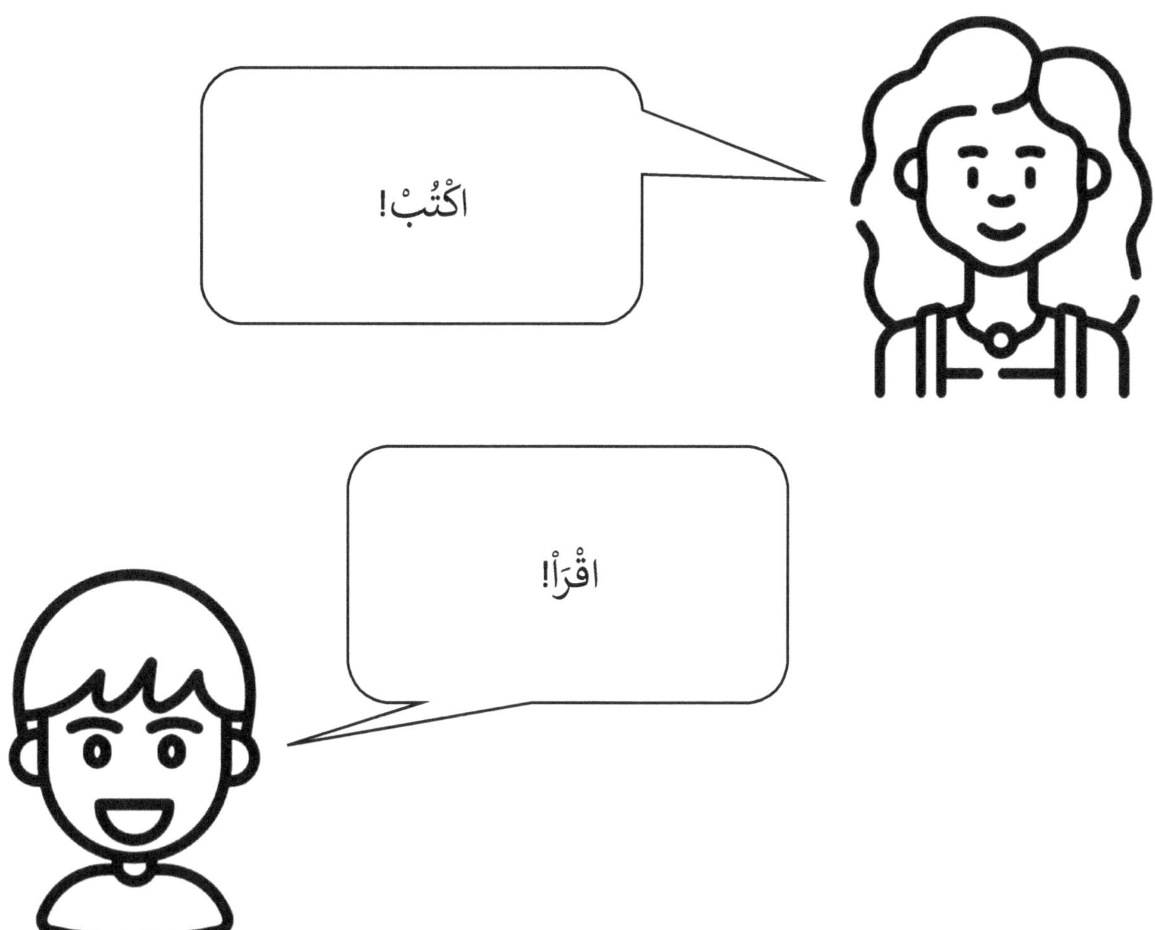

1. Listen and repeat the following words with sukoon. 🔊

أُثْ	إِثْ	أَثْ	أُتْ	إِتْ	أَتْ	أُبْ	إِبْ	أَبْ
أُخْ	إِخْ	أَخْ	بُحْ	بِحْ	بَحْ	بُجْ	بِجْ	بَجْ
مُرْ	مِرْ	مَرْ	أُذْ	إِذْ	أَذْ	سُدْ	سِدْ	سَدْ
أُشْ	إِشْ	أَشْ	أُسْ	إِسْ	أَسْ	أُزْ	إِزْ	أَزْ
أُظْ	إِظْ	أَظْ	أُضْ	إِضْ	أَضْ	أُصْ	إِصْ	أَصْ
أُغْ	إِغْ	أَغْ	تُعْ	تِعْ	تَعْ	أُظْ	إِظْ	أَظْ
أُكْ	إِكْ	أَكْ	أُقْ	إِقْ	أَقْ	أُفْ	إِفْ	أَفْ
أُنْ	إِنْ	أَنْ	لُمْ	لِمْ	لَمْ	أُلْ	إِلْ	أَلْ
-	-	أَيْ	-	-	أُوْ	أُهْ	إِهْ	أَهْ

THE LANGUAGE GYM

2. Listen, read along and copy the following words with sukoon.

خُذْ	جُدْ	تُبْ	بِعْ	بِتْ	بَلْ	أَنْ	أَخْ	.١ wāhid
صِلْ	سُدْ	سِرْ	سَلْ	زِنْ	زِدْ	ذُقْ	دَعْ	.٢ ithnān
عِشْ	عِظْ	عَنْ	طِرْ	طِبْ	ضَعْ	صُمْ	صُنْ	.٣ thalātha
نَمْ	قُمْ	قِسْ	قِفْ	قَدْ	فُزْ	غِبْ	عُدْ	.٤ arb'a
مَنْ	لَكْ	لَمْ	لَوْ	لَنْ	كُنْ	كُلْ	كَيْ	.٥ khamsa

صَوْتُ	ظُهْرُ	عَصْرُ	فَجْرُ	مِصْرُ	نَحْنُ	.٦ sitta
غَرْبُ	شَرْقُ	عَذْبُ	حَرْفُ	وَقْفُ	سَطْرُ	.٧ sab'a

<table>
<tr><td>يُرْسِلُ</td><td>يُسْلِمُ</td><td>يَخْرُجُ</td><td>أَشْرَكَ</td><td>أَبْصَرَ</td><td>أَتْقَنَ</td><td>١.
wāhid</td></tr>
<tr><td>............</td><td>............</td><td>............</td><td>............</td><td>............</td><td>............</td><td></td></tr>
<tr><td>تَعْبُدُ</td><td>تَشْكُرُ</td><td>تَدْمَعُ</td><td>نَحْمَدُ</td><td>نَسْجُدُ</td><td>نَرْكَعُ</td><td>٢.
ithnān</td></tr>
<tr><td>............</td><td>............</td><td>............</td><td>............</td><td>............</td><td>............</td><td></td></tr>
<tr><td>أَسْمِعُ</td><td>أَنْصِتُ</td><td>أَقْبِلْ</td><td>أَسْلِمْ</td><td>أَيْقِظْ</td><td>أَرْسِلْ</td><td>٣.
thalātha</td></tr>
<tr><td>............</td><td>............</td><td>............</td><td>............</td><td>............</td><td>............</td><td></td></tr>
</table>

<table>
<tr><td>لَنْ أَظْلِمَ بَلْ أَعْدِلَ</td><td>لَنْ نَكْذِبَ بَلْ نَصْدُقَ</td><td>٤.
arb'a</td></tr>
<tr><td>............</td><td>............</td><td></td></tr>
<tr><td>لَنْ أَسْرِقَ لَنْ أَحْلِفَ كَذِبًا</td><td>لَنْ أَطْمَعَ بَلْ أَقْنَعَ</td><td>٥.
khamsa</td></tr>
<tr><td>............</td><td>............</td><td></td></tr>
<tr><td colspan="2">ضَعْ قَلَمَكَ وَقُلْ دَرْسَكَ كَيْ تَنْجَحَ</td><td>٦.
sitta</td></tr>
<tr><td colspan="2">............</td><td></td></tr>
</table>

UNIT 4

التنوين

In this unit you will learn:

- ✓ The rules of tanween (nunation)
- ✓ The different suffixes of tanween

THE LANGUAGE GYM

1. Listen and repeat the following letters with tanween 🔊

حَاحٍحُ	جَاجٍجُ	ثَاثٍثُ	تَاتٍتُ	بَابٍبُ
زَازٍزُ	رَارٍرُ	ذَاذٍذُ	دَادٍدُ	خَاخٍخُ
طَاطٍطُ	ضَاضٍضُ	صَاصٍصُ	شَاشٍشُ	سَاسٍسُ
قَاقٍقُ	فَافٍفُ	غَاغٍغُ	عَاعٍعُ	ظَاظٍظُ
هَاهٍهُ	نَانٍنُ	مَامٍمُ	لَالٍلُ	كَاكٍكُ
	ةَاةٍةُ	يَايٍيُ	ءَءٍءُ	وَاوٍوُ

Fathataan فتحتان Listen, read along and copy 🔊

أَسَداً	فَرَحاً	بَطَلاً	غَداً	إذاً	أَباً	٠.١ wāhid
قَصَصاً	جَدَلاً	أَدَباً	وَسَطاً	خَلَقاً	أَحَداً	٢. ithnān
مَكْتَبَةً	مَدْرَسَةً	كُفُواً	غُرُفاً	عَدَداً	هُزُواً	٣. thalātha

Kasrataan كسرتان Listen, read along and copy 🔊

٠١ wāhid	بَطَلٍ	أَسَدٍ	بَشَرٍ	سُرُرٍ	كَذِبٍ	عَمَلٍ
	....	....	....	....	....	....
٠٢ ithnān	مَلَكٍ	جَبَلٍ	عَلَقٍ	خُلُقٍ	أُمَمٍ	كُتُبٍ
	....	....	....	....	....	....
٠٣ thalātha	خَشَبٍ	سُفُنٍ	كَلِمَةٍ	فِئَةٍ	هُمُزَةٍ	كَشَجَرَةٍ
	....	....	....	....	....	....

Dhammataan ضمتان Listen, read along and copy 🔊

٠١ wāhid	أَسَدٌ	بَطَلٌ	وَرَقٌ	قَلَمٌ	صِلَةٌ	مَطَرٌ
	....	....	....	....	....	....
٠٢ ithnān	رُسُلٌ	عُنُقٌ	قَسَمٌ	عِنَبٌ	شُهُبٌ	نُسُكٌ
	....	....	....	....	....	....
٠٣ thalātha	طُرُقٌ	ثُلُثٌ	بَرَكَةٌ	حَشَرَةٌ	قَتَرَةٌ	غَبَرَةٌ
	....	....	....	....	....	....

Bringing it all together: read and then write the following phrases that include vowels (harakaat), sukoon and tanween!

دَعْ جَهْلاً	خُذْ عِلْماً	**.١** wāhid
نَمْ لَيْلاً	قُمْ صُبْحاً	**.٢** ithnān
سَلْ نَصْراً	خَفْ ذَنْباً	**.٣** thalātha
فُزْ أَبَداً	تُبْ دَوْماً	**.٤** arb'a
كُلْ فِطْراً	صُمْ شَهْراً	**.٥** khamsa
عِظْ قَوْماً	قُلْ قَوْلاً	**.٦** sitta
بِتْ فَرْحاً	ذَرْ ظُلْماً	**.٧** sab'a
طُلْ عُمْراً	صِلْ رَحِماً	**.٨** thamāniya

سُعْ خُلُقاً	جُدْ خَيْراً	.٩ tis'a
....	....	
نَلْ قَدْراً	ضَعْ كِبْراً	.١٠ 'ashara
....	....	

			.١ wāhid
			.٢ ithnān
			.٣ thalātha
			.٤ arb'a
			.٥ khamsa
			.٦ sitta
			.٧ sab'a
			.٨ thamāniya

THE LANGUAGE GYM

UNIT 4 - ANSWERS – Nunation – The 'an', 'in' 'un' sounds.

2. Listen and write out the following words and phrases that are being said

أُمَمٍ	كُتُبٍ	كَلِمَةٍ	.١ **wāhid**
شَجَرَةٌ	بَشَرٍ	أَسَدٍ	.٢ **ithnān**
قَسَمٌ	بَرَكَةٌ	ثُلُثٌ	.٣ **thalātha**
قَصَصاً	مَطَرٌ	صِلَةٌ	.٤ **arb'a**
أَباً	مَدْرَسَةً	كُفُواً	.٥ **khamsa**
أَدَباً	وَسَطاً	خَلَقاً	.٦ **sitta**
	جُدْ خَيْراً		.٧ **sab'a**
	قُلْ قَوْلاً		.٨ **thamāniya**

UNIT 5

المدود

In this unit you will learn:

1. The long vowels

THE LANGUAGE GYM

1. Listen and repeat the following letters with a fatha and then with a fatha and stretched alif. 🔊

جَا	جَ	ثَا	ثَ	تَا	تَ	بَا	بَ	آ	أَ
رَا	رَ	ذَا	ذَ	دَا	دَ	خَا	خَ	حَا	حَ
ضَا	ضَ	صَا	صَ	شَا	شَ	سَا	سَ	زَا	زَ
فَا	فَ	غَا	غَ	عَا	عَ	ظَا	ظَ	طَا	طَ
نَا	نَ	مَا	مَ	لَا	لَ	كَا	كَ	قَا	قَ
		يَا	يَ	ءَا	ءَ	وَا	وَ	هَا	هَ

حَانَ	جَاعَ	ثَارَ	تَابَ	بَابٌ	آبَ	١. wāhid
....	....	....	....	....	....	
سَالَ	زَادَ	رَامَ	ذَاقَ	دَارٌ	خَافَ	٢. ithnān
....	....	....	....	....	....	
فَازَ	عَادَ	طَارَ	ضَاعَ	صَاحَ	شَانَ	٣. thalātha
....	....	....	....	....	....	
هَانَ	نَامَ	مَاتَ	لَامَ	كَانَ	قَالَ	٤. arb'a
....	....	....	....	....	....	

THE LANGUAGE GYM

٥. khamsa	بَارَكَ	جَاهَدَ	حَاكَمَ	عَامَلَ	شَاهَدَ	نَاصَرَ
٦. sitta	بَنَاهَا	تَلَاهَا	ضُحَاهَا	تَعَامَلَ	ضَرَبَا	ضَرَبَنَا
٧. sab'a	ضَرَبَتَا	قَمَرَانِ	يُشَاهِدَانِ	قَلَمَانِ	كِتَابَانِ	صَفَحَاتٍ
٨. thamāniya	عِظَامَهُ	بَنَانَهُ	حَدَائِقَ	إِمَامَنَا	فَسَامَحَهُ	عَلَامَةً
٩. tis'a	عَاصِمَةٌ	لِمَاذَا	أَمَامَ	وَبَرَكَاتُهُ	أَبْوَاب	آدَاب
١٠. 'ashara	أَطَالَ	أَقَاطِعُ	رَآهَا	فَقَامَ	قَائِد	دُعَاءَ

١١. ihda'ashara	تُسَافِرَانِ	يُمَارِسُ	يُذَاكِرَانِ	مَدَارِسُنَا

١٢. ithna'ashara	أَقَابِلُ زَائِرَنَا	يُطَالِعُ كِتَابَهُ	تُذَاكِرُ لَكُمَا

١٣.	تَابَ وَرَفَعَ يَدَهُ وَدَعَا	أَجَابَ دُعَاءَهُ خَالِقُهُ

1A. Listen and repeat the following letters with 'alif maqsura'

هَدَى	رَمَى	بَنَى	رَأَى	إِلَى	عَلَى	**.١** wāhid
....	....	....	....	....	....	
يَرْضَى	أَلْقَى	عَسَى	حَتَّى	مَضَى	مَتَى	**.٢** ithnān
....	....	....	....	....	....	
أُخْرَى	تَعَالَى	لِيَبْقَى	اِشْتَرَى	لِيَرَى	قُرْبَى	**.٣** thalātha
....	....	....	....	....	....	

THE LANGUAGE GYM

عَلِمَ 'alima
عَلِيم a'leem

قَصِرَ qasira
قَصِيرَ qaseera

2. Listen and repeat the following letters with a 'kasra' and then with a 'kasra and stretched yaa'. 🔊

إِ	إِي	بِ	بِي	تِ	تِي	ثِ	ثِي	جِ	جِي
حِ	حِي	خِ	خِي	دِ	دِي	ذِ	ذِي	رِ	رِي
زِ	زِي	سِ	سِي	شِ	شِي	صِ	صِي	ضِ	ضِي
طِ	طِي	ظِ	ظِي	عِ	عِي	غِ	غِي	فِ	فِي
قِ	قِي	كِ	كِي	لِ	لِي	مِ	مِي	نِ	نِي
هِ	هِي	وِ	وِي	ءِ	ءِي	يِ	يِي		

لُغَتِي	تِي	طَبِيبٌ	بِي	إِيمَانًا	إي
رَيَاحِينُ	حِي	عَجِيبٌ	جِي	ثِيرَانُ	ثِي
مُذِيعٌ	ذِي	حَدِيقَةٌ	دِي	أَخِي	خِي
نَسِيمٌ	سِي	أَزِيزٌ	زِي	جَارِي	رِي
فَضِيلَةٌ	ضِي	عَصِيرٌ	صِي	بَشِيرًا	شِي
سَعِيدٌ	عِي	نَظِيفٌ	ظِي	يَطِيرُ	طِي
حَقِيبَةٌ	قِي	فِيهَا	فِي	صَغِيرٌ	غِي
زَمِيلَةٌ	مِي	بَلِيغٌ	لِي	يَشْتَكِي	كِي
طَوِيلٌ	وِي	يُبَاهِي	هِي	مَعَانِي	نِي
		مَعَايِيرُ	يِ		

قِيلَ	صِيدَ	فِيهِ	زِيدَ	حِينَ	بِيعَ	١. wāhid
....	....	....	....	....	....	
مَدِينَةَ	حَدِيثُ	جَدِيدُ	طَرِيقُ	أُعِيدُ	أُقِيمُ	٢. ithnān
....	....	....	....	....	....	
خُلُقِي	وَطَنِي	تَلَامِيذُ	لِسَانِي	كِتَابِي	بِلَادِي	٣. thalātha
....	....	....	....	....	....	
وَقِيلَ	مَصِيفُ	جَزِيرَةُ	بَسَاتِيْنُ	كَثِيرَةَ	رَيَاحِينُ	٤. arb'a
....	....	....	....	....	....	

<table>
<tr><td colspan="2">Info box: when a 'waw' و is added to a letter with a 'dhammah' ُ then the letter will be stretched:</td></tr>
<tr><td>rusoolun</td><td></td><td>رُسُولٌ</td><td>rusulun</td><td>رُسُلٌ</td></tr>
</table>

3. Listen and repeat the following letters with a 'dhammah' and then with a 'dhammah and stretched wāw'

جُو	جُ	ثُو	ثُ	تُو	تُ	بُو	بُ	أُو	أُ
رُو	رُ	ذُو	ذُ	دُو	دُ	خُو	خُ	حُو	حُ
ضُو	ضُ	صُو	صُ	شُو	شُ	سُو	سُ	زُو	زُ
فُو	فُ	غُو	غُ	عُو	عُ	ظُو	ظُ	طُو	طُ
نُو	نُ	مُو	مُ	لُو	لُ	كُو	كُ	قُو	قُ
		يُو	يُ	ءُو	ءُ	وُو	وُ	هُو	هُ

3A Listen and practise these letters with all three stretched vowels

جَا جِي جُو	ثَا ثِي ثُو	تَا تِي تُو	بَا بِي بُو	آ إِي أُو
زَا زِي رُو	ذَا ذِي ذُو	دَا دِي دُو	خَا خِي خُو	حَا حِي حُو
ضَا ضِي ضُو	صَا صِي صُو	شَا شِي شُو	سَا سِي سُو	زَا زِي زُو
فَا فِي فُو	غَا غِي غُو	عَا عِي عُو	ظَا ظِي ظُو	طَا طِي طُو
نَا نِي نُو	مَا مِي مُو	لَا لِي لُو	كَا كِي كُو	قَا قِي قُو
		يَا يِي يُو	وَا وِي وُو	هَا هِي هُو

أُو	أُولَى	بُو	رُبُوعِ	تُو	تُوجَدُ
ثُو	يَعْبَثُونَ	جُو	وُجُوهٌ	حُو	لُحُومٌ
خُو	خُوخٌ	دُو	صُنْدُوقٌ	ذُو	بُذُورٌ
رُو	عَرُوسَ	زُو	تَزُورُ	سُو	تَسُودُ
شُو	يَعِيشُونَ	صُو	صُورَةً	ضُو	وُضُوءٌ
طُو	فُطُورُكَ	ظُو	مَنْظُورٌ	عُو	سُعُودٌ
غُو	يَغُوصُ	فُو	عُصْفُورٌ	قُو	أَقُولُ
كُو	سَتَكُونُ	لُو	مُلُوكٌ	مُو	يَنَامُوا
نُو	كَنُوزٌ	هُو	سُهُولَةٌ	وُو	طَاوُوسٌ
		يُو	يُوسُفُ		

.١ wāhid	أَبُوكَ	أَتُوبُ	أَفُوزُ	أَقُولُ	أَزُورُ	أَطُوفُ
.٢ ithnān	يَرْجُو	يَنْمُو	يَشْكُو	يَدْعُو	يَبْدُو	يَبْلُو
.٣ thalātha	لَعِبُوا	شَرِبُوا	أَكَلُوا	عَبَدُوا	نَجَحُوا	سَمِعُوا
.٤ arb'a	تَابُوا	جَاهَدُوا	عَامَلُوا	نَامُوا	شَاهَدُوا	بَاعُوا
.٥ khamsa	قَالُوا	يَقُولُوا	تَقُولُونَ	كَانُوا	يَكُونُوا	تَكُونُونَ
.٦ sitta	سَبَقُوا	سَبَقُونَا	سَابِقُونَ	عَلِمُوا	عَالِمُونَ	يَعْلَمُونَ

4. Listen and write out the following words and phrases that are being said 

.١ wāhid			
.٢ ithnān			
.٣ thalātha			

THE LANGUAGE GYM

UNIT 5 - ANSWERS – The Long Vowels – The 'aa', 'ee' 'oo' sounds.

4. Listen and write out the following words and phrases that are being said

تَسُودُ	أَكَلُوا	رُبُوعِ	١. wāhid
أَقُولُ	يَعِيشُونَ	لِسَاني	٢. ithnān
عَلَى	أَلَقَى	تَلَامِيذُ	٣. thalātha

UNIT 6

الحرف المشدَّد

In this unit you will learn:

✓ How to pronounce and read letters with a 'shadda' on them.

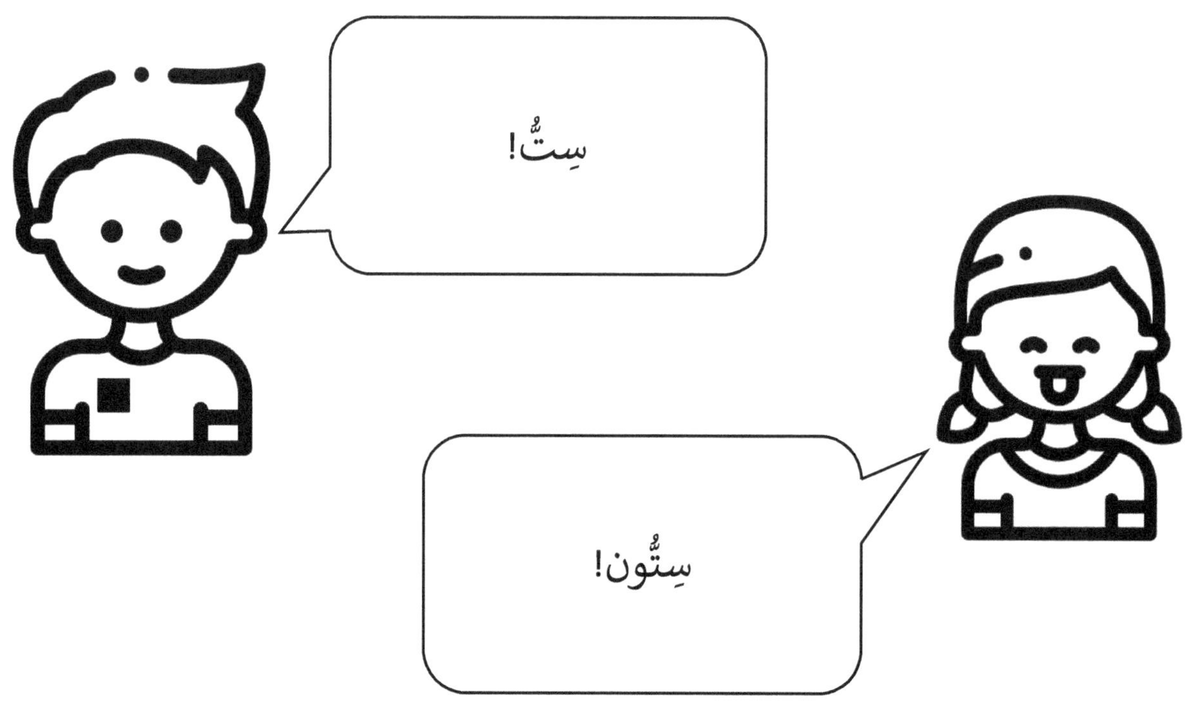

	أُبّ			أِبّ			أَبّ	
بُ	+	أبْ	بِ	+	أبْ	بَ	+	أبْ
ab + bu			ab + bi			ab + ba		

1. Listen and repeat the following letters with shaddah 🔊

أَبّ	أَبّ	أَبّ	إِبّ	إِبّ	إِبّ	أُبّ	أُبّ	أُبّ
حَجّ	حَجّ	حَجّ	إِجّ	إِجّ	إِجّ	أُجّ	أُجّ	أُجّ
عَزّ	عَزّ	عَزّ	إِزّ	إِزّ	إِزّ	أُزّ	أُزّ	أُزّ
مَسّ	مَسّ	مَسّ	إِسّ	إِسّ	إِسّ	أُسّ	أُسّ	أُسّ
أَظّ	أَظّ	أَظّ	إِظّ	إِظّ	إِظّ	أُظّ	أُظّ	أُظّ
أَعّ	أَعّ	أَعّ	إِعّ	إِعّ	إِعّ	أُعّ	أُعّ	أُعّ
أَكّ	أَكّ	أَكّ	إِكّ	إِكّ	إِكّ	دُكّ	دُكّ	دُكّ
أَنّ	أَنّ	أَنّ	إِنّ	إِنّ	إِنّ	أُنّ	أُنّ	أُنّ
أَوّ	أَوّ	أَوّ	سِوّ	سِوّ	سِوّ	قُوّ	قُوّ	قُوّ
أَيّ	أَيّ	أَيّ	إِيّ	إِيّ	إِيّ	حُيّ	حُيّ	حُيّ

.١ wāhid	صَبَّ	بَتَّ	حَثَّ	حَجَّ	صَعَّ	ذَمَّ
	صَبْ/بَ	..../....	..../....	..../....	..../....	..../....
	صَبَّ	....	....	....	....	....
.٢ ithnān	شَدَّ	دَلَّ	رَشَّ	قَصَّ	قَطَّ	دُكَّ
	..../....	..../....	..../....	..../....	..../....	..../....
	....	....	....	....	....	....
.٣ thalātha	رُبَّ	ثُمَّ	فَرَّ	دُسَّ	عَمِّي	أُمِّي
	..../....	..../....	..../....	..../....	..../....	..../....
	....	....	....	....	....	....

.٤ arb'a	صَدَّكَ	حَذَّرَ	كَرَّمَ	فَكَّرَ	عَظَّمَ
	صَدْ/دَ/كَ	..../..../...	..../..../...	..../..../...	..../..../...
	صَدَّكَ	....	....	....	....
.٥ khamsa	خُيِّرَ	طُهِّرَ	حُبِّبَ	رُتِّبَ	بُشِّرَ
	..../..../...	..../..../...	..../..../...	..../..../...	..../..../...
	....	....	....	....	....
.٦ sitta	يَقُصُّ	يَدُلُّ	يَوَدُّ	يَفِرُّ	يُحِبُّ
	..../..../...	..../..../...	..../..../...	..../..../...	..../..../...
	....	....	....	....	....

سُبْحَا	سَبَّحُوا	سَبَّحْنَا	سَبَّحْتَ	سَبَّحَ	.٧ sab'a
………………	………………	………………	………………	………………	
رَتَّبْنَا	رُتِّبَ	رَتَّبُوا	رَتَّبْتُ	رَتَّبَ	.٨ thamāniya
………………	………………	………………	………………	………………	
أَتَذَكَّرُ	يَتَذَكَّرانِ	تَتَذَكَّرْنَ	يَتَذَكَّرونَ	يَتَذَكَّرُ	.٩ tis'a
………………	………………	………………	………………	………………	

2. Listen and write out the following words and phrases that are being said 🔊

………………	………………	………………	.١ wāhid
………………	………………	………………	.٢ ithnān
………………	………………	………………	.٣ thalātha
			.٤ arb'a

THE LANGUAGE GYM

UNIT 6 - ANSWERS – Ash-shaddah – the doubling of letters

2. Listen and write out the following words and phrases that are being said

عَلَّمْتُ	عَلَّمُوا	عَلَّمَ	.١ **wāhid**
دَرَّسْتُمْ	دَرَّسْنَ	دَرَّسَ	.٢ **ithnān**
أَصُبُّ	نَصُبُّ	يَصُبُّ	.٣ **thalātha**
تَتَكَلَّمَانِ	يَتَكَلَّمُونَ	أَتكَلَّمُ	.٤ **arb'a**

THE LANGUAGE GYM

UNIT 7

اللام الشمسية واللام القمرية

In this unit you will learn:

- ✓ The sun letters
- ✓ The moon letters
- ✓ The connecting hamza الهمزة الوصل
- ✓ The fixed hamza الهمزة القطع

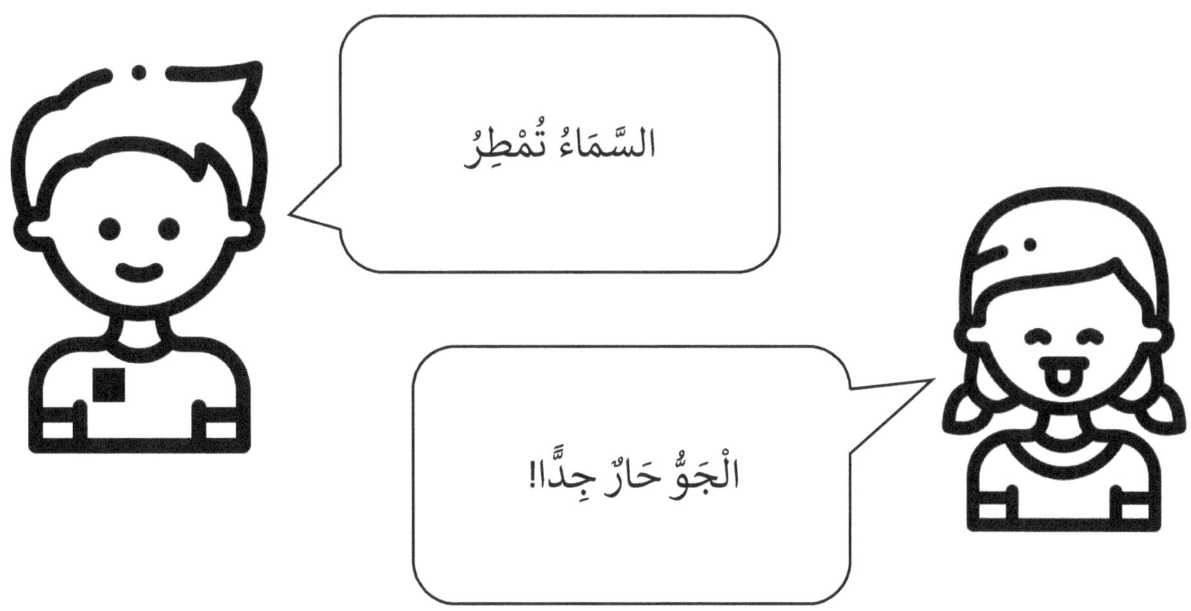

Info box: When the letters 'alif' & 'laam' are at the beginning of a noun we add 'the' when translating into English. The word will also be pronounced differently depending on the letter after the 'laam' at the beginning.

If the following letters come after a 'laam' at the beginning of a word:

أ-ب-ج-ح-خ-ع-غ-ف-ق-ك-م-و-ه-ي

... then we add a sukoon on the 'laam', pronouncing it and the letter after:

الكتاب > اَلْكِتاب > al kitaab

الاسم	الْ + الحرف	الاسم	الْ + الحرف
الْبَابُ	الْ + بَ	الْأَخْلَاقُ	الْ + أ
....	....	....	الأ
الْحَدِيثَ	الْ + حَ	الْجَارُ	الْ + جَ
....	....	....	....
الْعَيْنُ	الْ + عَ	الْخَيْرُ	الْ + خَ
....	....	....	....
الْفَصْلُ	ال + فِ	الْغَائِبُ	الْ + غَ
....	....	....	....
الْكِتَابُ	ال + ك	الْقَلْبُ	الْ + قَ
....	....	....	....
الْوَالِدُ	ال + و	الْمَسْجِدَ	الْ + مَ
....	....	....	....
الْيَمِيْنُ	ال + يِ	الْهِلَالُ	الْ + هَ
....	....	....	....

Info box: The sun letters – اللام الشمسية

If the following letters come after a 'laam' at the beginning of a word:

ت-ث-د-ذ-ر-ز-س-ش-ص-ض-ط-ظ-ل-ن

...then we **don't** pronounce the 'laam'. Instead we add a 'shaddah' on the letter after the 'laam' and pronounce it as such:

السماء > اَلسَّمَاءُ > as samaau

الاسم	الْ + الحرف	الاسم	الْ + الحرف
الثَّالِثُ	الثَّ	التَّلَامِيذُ	التَّ
....	....	....	....
الذِّئْبُ	الذِّ	الدِّرَاسِيَّ	الدِّ
....	....	....	....
الزِّينَةُ	الزِّ	الرَّسُولُ	الرَّ
....	....	....	....
الشَّارِعُ	الشَّ	السَّفَرِ	السَّ
....	....	....	....
الضَّابِطُ	الضَّ	الصَّفَّ	الصَّ
....	....	....	....
الظَّلَامُ	الظَّ	الطَّائِرَةِ	الطَّ
....	....	....	....
النَّدَاءَ	النَّ	اللَّوْنَ	اللَّ
....	....	....	....

أَرْجُوْ	أَفْعَلُ	أَبْلِغْ	أَزُوْرُهُ
....	....	....	....

فِي الرَّابِعِ	فِي الْخَامِسِ	صَبَاحُ الْخَيْرِ	بِالدَّفَاعِ
....	....	....	....

UNIT 8

اسمي وعمري

In this unit you will learn:

- ✓ How to say 'my name is ...'
- ✓ How to say 'my age is ...'
- ✓ The numbers 1-12 in Arabic

THE LANGUAGE GYM

UNIT 8 اسمي وعمري
I can say my name and my age

> مَا اسْمُك؟ *What's your name?*
> كَمْ عُمْرُك؟ *How old are you?*

وَاحِدَة **one**	سَنَةٌ **year**			Ibraahim إِبْرَاهِيم		مَرْحَبا **Hello!**
	سَنَتَان **two years**			Bilaal بِلَال		
	ثَلَاثُ ٣ 3			Jamaal جَمَال		
	أَرْبَعُ ٤ 4			Hasan حَسَن		صَباحُ الخَيْر! **Good morning!**
	خَمْسُ ٥ 5			Zaynab رَيْنَب	إِسْمِي **My name is**	
سَنَوَات **years**	سِتُّ ٦ 6	عُمْرِي **my age is**	وَ **and**	Safiyyah صَفِيَّة	أَنَا **I am**	مَساءُ الخَيْر! **Good afternoon!**
	سَبْعُ ٧ 7			'Aisha عَائِشَة		
	ثَمَانِي ٨ 8			'Umar عُمَر		
	تِسْعُ ٩ 9			Maryam مَرْيَم		
	عَشْرُ ١٠ 10			Hind هِنْد		
سَنَة **years**	إِحْدَى عَشْرَةَ ١١ 11					
	اِثْنَتَا عَشْرَةَ ١٢ 12					

Unit 8. My name and age: LISTENING

1. Complete with the missing syllables in the box below

a. Hello!	ا. مرحـ______
b. Good morning	ب. صبـ______ الخير
c. I am 5 years old	ت. عمري ______س سنوات
d. My name is	ث. ______ي
e. Eleven years	ث. إحدى عشـ___ة
f. Good evening	ج. مساء ________
الخير اسم با خم ر اح	

2. Can you help the penguin to break the flow?

مثال: مرحباسميأحمدوعمريعشرسنوات
مرحبا اسمي أحمد وعمري عشر سنوات
ا. صباحالخيراسميسلماعمريخمسسنوات
ب. مساء الخيراسميزينبوعمريسبعسنوات.
ت. مرحباسميمحمودوعمرياًحدىعشرةسنة
ث. صباح الخيراسميجمالوعمريتسعسنوات
ج. اسمييوسفوعمريستسنوات

3. Listen and circle the correct number (1-12)

(٧)	(٨)	◯	مثال
ستّ (٦)	سبع (٧)	ثماني (٨)	ا.
عشر (١٠)	ثلاث (٣)	سنتان (٢)	ب.
تسع (٩)	اثنتا عشرة (١٢)	إحدى عشرة (١١)	ت.
أربع (٤)	خمس (٥)	واحدة (١)	ث.
اثنتا عشرة (١٢)	ست (٦)	أربع (٤)	ج.

4. Spelling Challenge (1-12)
Listen and complete the words with the missing letter

a.	اثنا__	g.	ث__اني
b.	واح__	h.	ث__ث
c.	__ت	i.	أر__ع
d.	ت__ع	j.	سب__
e.	خ__س	k.	إح__ى عش__ة
f.	ع__ر	l.	اثن__ا ع__رة

THE LANGUAGE GYM

5. Listen and fill in the grid with the correct name and age

	Name	Age
a.		
b.		
c.		
d.		

6. Listen and tick one option

1	2	3	
إحسان	أسد	آدم	ا.
مريم	عائشة	فاطمة	ب.
أربع سنوات	إحدى عشرة سنة	سنتان	ت.
ثماني سنوات	عشر سنوات	اثنتا عشرة سنة	ث.
ما اسمك؟	صباح الخير	كم عمرك؟	ج.

THE LANGUAGE GYM

7. Faulty Echo

Identify and underline the word in Arabic that is pronounced incorrectly in each sentence

مثال: <u>عمري</u> ست سنوات.
ا. اسمي عائشة
ب. مرحبا! عمري خمس سنوات
ت. صباح الخير! اسمي مريم
ث. مرحبا! اسمي بلال وعمري ثماني سنوات
ج. اسمي هند وعمري خمس سنوات

8. Spot the Intruder

Identify and underline the word in each sentence the speaker is NOT saying

مثال: <u>اسمي</u> موسى <u>مرحبا</u>
ا. ما اسمك؟ ليس اسمي نورا
ب. كم عمرك؟ عمري ست ثلاث سنوات
ت. مرحبا، خمس اسمي هوما
ث. مساء الخير، عمري اسمي محمد

Unit 8. My name and age: WORD BUILDING
Practise hand writing the following words

						اسمي	اسمي
						أنا	أنا
						عمري	عمري
						سنة	سنة
						سنتان	سنتان
						سنوات	سنوات
						واحدة	واحدة
						ثلاث	ثلاث
						أربع	أربع
						خمس	خمس
						ست	ست
						سبع	سبع
						ثماني	ثماني

Unit 8. My name and age: VOCABULARY BUILDING

1. Match Up

a. Ten	ا. اسمي	a	
b. Four	ب. أربع	b	
c. Two	ت. سنوات	c	
d. Five	ث. سبع	d	
e. My name is	ج. ثلاث	e	
f. Seven	ح. إحدى عشرة	f	
g. Three	خ. اثنان	g	
h. Thirteen	د. عشر	h	
i. Years	ذ. خمس	i	
j. Eleven	ر. ثلاث عشرة	j	

2. Missing Words 

a. *My age is* _______

b. *Six* _______

c. *Years* _______

d. *My name is* _______

e. *One* _______

f. *Ten* _______

عمري	عشر
ست	واحد
سنوات	اسمي

3. Complete the sentences with the missing words below

I am **seven** years old.	ا. عمري _______ سنوات
My name is Anas.	ب. _______ أنس
I am **eleven** years old.	ت. عمري _______ _______ سنة
What is your name?	ث. ___ اسمك؟
What **age** are you?	ج. كم ___ك؟
Hello, my name is **Maryam**.	ح. مرحبا، اسمي ___
I am **eight** years old.	خ. عمري _______ سنوات
My name is Hind, and I am **13**.	د. اسمي هند وعمري _______ عشرة سنة

مريم	إحدى عشرة	سبع	ثماني	عمر	اسمي	ما	ثلاث

THE LANGUAGE GYM

Unit 8. My name and age: WORD BUILDING

4. Sentence Building Blocks
Use the words in the building blocks to make a correct Arabic sentence

سنوات

عمري خمس

ا. ____________________

عمرك؟ كم

ب. ____________________

محمد اسمي اثنتا عشرة
سنة عمري و

ت. ____________________

اسمي إحدى بلال
سنة عمري و عشرة

ث. ____________________

Unit 8. My name and age: READING

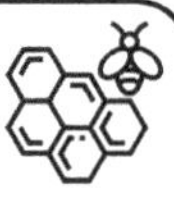

1. Sylla-Bees
Translate the phrases putting the cells in the correct order

a. *My name is Sulaimaan.*

____

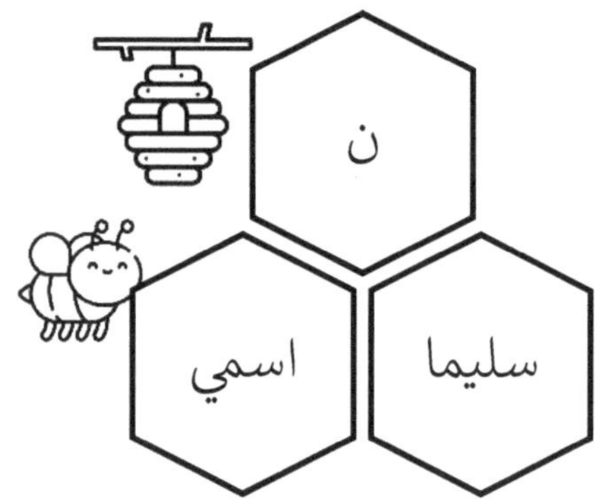

b. *I am 9 years old.*

____

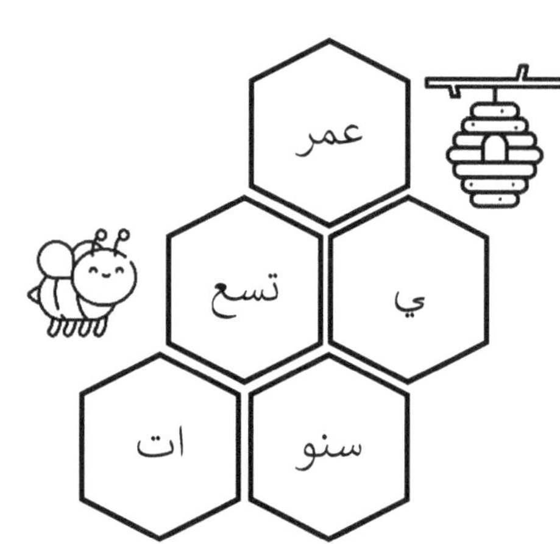

c. *I am 6 years old.*

____

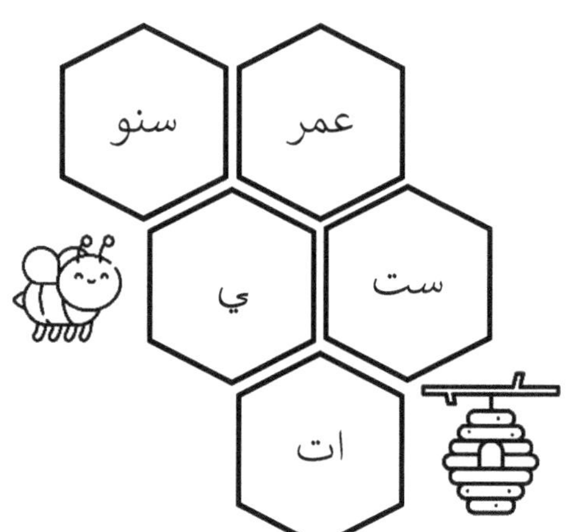

THE LANGUAGE GYM

2. True or False ✓
Read the dialogues below and for each statement tick

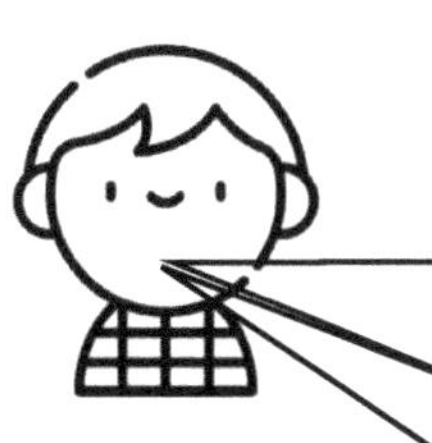

	True	False
1a. Her name is A'isha.		
1b. His name is Muhammad		
1c. She is 8 years old.		
1d. He is 11 years old.		
2a. Her name is Maryam.		
2b. His name is Zayn		
2c. She is 10 years old.		
2d. He is 12 years old.		

THE LANGUAGE GYM

1. Sentence Jumble

a. *I am 8 years old.*

ثماني عمري سنوات

b. *My name is Ruqaiyyah.*

رقية اسمي

c. *I am twelve years old.*

عشرة سنة اثنتا عمري

d. *I am seven years old.*

سنوات سبع عمري

e. *I am eleven years old.*

سنة عمري إحدى عشرة

2. Faulty Translation: write the correct English version

I am 10 years old	⇐ *I am __11__ years old.*	عمري عشر سنوات
	⇐ I am 6 years old.	عمري سبع سنوات
	⇐ What's your name?	كم عمرك؟
	⇐ Good evening	صباح الخير
	⇐ How old are you?	ما اسمك؟
	⇐ Bye, my name's Layla.	مرحبا، اسمي ليلى

3. Phrase-level Translation
How would you say it in Arabic?

a. I am 8 years old. ______________________________

b. My name is... ______________________________

c. What's your name? ______________________________

d. I am 12 years old. ______________________________

e. How old are you? ______________________________

f. Good morning. ______________________________

g. Hello. ______________________________

h. I am 9 years old. ______________________________

UNIT 8 - ANSWERS - اسمي و عمري (My name and age)

LISTENING

1. Listen and complete with the missing vowel

١. مرحبا ب. صباح الخير ت. عمري خمس سنوات. ث. اسمي   ج. إحدى عشرة سنة.

ح. مساء الخير.

2. Can you help the penguin to break the flow?

ا. مرحبا، اسمي سلمى وعمري خمس سنوات

ب. مساء الخير اسمي زينب، عمري سبع سنوات

ت. مرحبا، اسمي محمود وعمري إحدى عشرة سنة

ت. صباح الخير اسمي جمال وعمري تسع سنوات

ث. اسمي يوسف وعمري ست سنوات

3. Listen and circle the correct number

ا. عمري ست سنوات. ب. عمري ثلاث سنوات. ت. عمري اثنتا عشرة سنة. ث. عمري خمس سنوات. ج. عمري أربع سنوات

4. Complete with the missing syllables in the box below

ا. اثنان ب. واحد ت. ست. ث. تسع. ج. خمس. ح. عشر. خ. ثماني د. ثلاث. ذ. أربع ر. سبع ز. إحدى عشرة س. اثنتا عشرة

5. Fill in the grid with the correct name and age ✏

a. ismi Muhammad, u'mri khamsu sanawat

b. sabah ul khayr, ismi musa wa u'mri sittu sanawat

c. marhaban ismi Safiyyah wa u'mri ihda ashara

d. Masmuk? Ismi Bilal wa u'mri sabu' sanawat

Muhammad ; 5

Musa ; 6

Safiyyah ; 11

Bilal ; 7

6. Listen and tick one option for each sentence

ا. آدم ب. مريم ت. أربع سنوات ث. ثماني سنوات. ج. ما اسمك؟

7. Faulty Echo.

ا. اسمي عائشة. (عيشة) ب. مرحبا، عمري خمس سنوات (كمس) ت. صباح الخير، اسمي مريم (صبح) ث. مرحبا، اسمي بلال وعمري ثماني سنوات. (سماني) ج. اسمي هند وعمري خمس سنوات. (إزمي)

8. Spot the Intruder

ا. ما اسمك؟ اسمي نورا (ليس)

ب. كم عمرك؟ عمري ثلاث سنوات (ست)

ت. مرحبا، اسمي هوما(خمس)

ث. مساء الخير، اسمي محمد (عمري)

VOCABULARY BUILDING

1 . Match Up

a. د   b. ب   c. خ   d. ذ   e. ا   f. ث   g. ج   h. ر   i. ت   j. ح

2. Missing Words

a. عمري   **b.** ست   **c.** سنوات   **d.** اسمي   **e.** واحد   **f.** عشر

3. Complete the sentences with the missing words below

ا. عمري **سبع** سنوات

ب. **اسمي** أنس

ت. عمري **إحدى عشرة** سنة

ث. **ما** اسمك؟

ج. كم **عمرك**؟

ح. مرحبا، اسمي **مريم**

خ. عمري **ثماني** سنوات

د. اسمي هند وعمري ثلاث عشرة سنة

4. Sentence Building Blocks

ا. عمري خمس سنوات

ب. كم عمرك؟

ت. اسمي محمد وعمري اثنتا عشرة سنة

ث. اسمي بلال وعمري إحدى عشرة سنة

READING

1. Sylla-Bees

a . اسمي سليمان   **b.** عمري تسع سنوات   **c.** عمري ست سنوات

2. True or False

1a. True	1b. False (Hasan)	1c. True	1d. False (10)
2a. False (Fatimah)	2b. False (Zayd)	2c. False (11)	2d. True

WRITING

1. Sentence Jumble

a. عمري ثماني سنوات   **b.** اسمي رقية   **c.** عمري اثنتا عشرة سنة   **d.** عمري إحدى عشرة سنة

2. Faulty Translation

a. I am **7** years old.

b. **What's your age**?

c. Good morning

d. **What's your name**?

e. **Hello,** my name's Layla.

3. Phrase-level Translation

a. عمري ثماني سنوات

b. اسمي

c. ما اسمك؟

d. عمري اثنتا عشر سنة

e. كم عمرك؟

f. صباح الخير

g. مرحبا

h. عمري تسع سنوات

> **In this unit you will learn how to say in Arabic:**
>
> ✓ How you are
>
> **You will revisit:**
>
> ★ What is your name
> ★ Saying your age
> ★ 'Hello' and 'Good morning'

THE LANGUAGE GYM

UNIT 9. كيف حالك؟
I can greet and say how I am

كَيْفَ حَالُكِ؟ *How are you?*

FEM	MASC		FEM	MASC		
			بِخَيْر *fine*	بِخَيْر *fine*		مَرْحبا *Hello*
مُتْعَبَة *tired*	مُتْعَب *tired*		طَيِّبة *good*	طَيِّب *good*		صَبَاحُ الْخَيْر *Good morning*
مُبْتَهِجة *cheerful*	مُبْتَهِج *cheerful*	لِأَنَّني *because I am*	بِأَحْسَنِ حَال *well*	بِأَحْسَنِ حَال *well*		مَسَاءُ الْخَيْر *Good afternoon*
مَضْغُوطَة *stressed*	مَضْغُوط *stressed*				أَنَا *I am*	لَيْلَة سَعِيدَة *Good evening / Good night*
سَعِيدَة *happy*	سَعِيد *happy*		جَيِّدَة *okay*	جَيِّد *okay*		
مُتَوَتِّرَة *nervous*	مُتَوَتِّر *nervous*	لَكِنَّني *however I am*				
مُرْتَاحَة *relaxed*	مُرْتَاح *relaxed*		لَسْتُ بِأَحْسَنِ حَال *not well*	لَسْتُ بِأَحْسَنِ حَال *not well*		شُكْرًا *Thank you*
هَادِئَة *calm*	هَادِئ *calm*					
حَزِينَة *sad*	حَزِين *sad*					

THE LANGUAGE GYM

1. Listen and tick the word you hear ✓

3	2	1	
صباح الخير	مرحبا	مساء الخير	مثال:
لست بأحسن حال	طيب	بخير	ا.
هادئة	حزين	هادئ	ب.
مبتهج	متعب	مبتهجة	ت.
متعب	بأحسن حال	متعبة	ث.
مضغوط	مضغوطة	سعيد	ج.

2. Listen and add the correct vowels (tashkeel)

a – ◌َ	د. مرحبا، اسمي موسى	ا. أنا مبتهج
an – ◌ً	ذ. أنا جيد جدا	ب. ليلة سعيدة
i – ◌ِ		
u – ◌ُ	ر. صباح الخير	ت. أنا هادئ
stop on the letter – ◌ْ	ز. أنا طيب	ث. مساء الخير
doubling of the letter – ◌ّ	س. أنا مرتاحة	ج. أنا بأحسن حال
	ش. أنا متوتر	ح. أنا حزين
	ص. أنا مضغوط	خ. أنا متعب

3. Complete with the missing syllables in the box below

ح. أنا بخير ____ني سعيدة	ا. أنا مض____
خ. أنا م____ج	ب. أ__ جيد
د. م____ا، اسمي عمر	ت. ص____ الخير
ذ. أنا متع____	ث. م____ الخير
ر. أنا ____ت بأحسن حال لأني متوتر	ج. أنا لست ب____ن حال

غوط	لس	بته	ساء	أحس	لأذ	باح	رحب	بة	نا

4. Listen and choose the correct spelling

A	B	
صباح الخير	سباح الخير	١.
أنا	أن	٢.
مساء الخير	مسا الخير	٣.
متعبة	متعبت	٤.
بخير	بكير	٥.
سعيد	سأيد	٦.
مدغوت	مضغوط	٧.
هزين	حزين	٨.
قيف حالك؟	كيف حالك؟	٩.
هادئة	هادئ	١٠.

THE LANGUAGE GYM

5. Break the flow: Separate the words and write out the sentences correctly underneath

‏ا. أنابخيرلأننيمبتهج
‏ب. أنالستبأحسنحاللأننيمتعبة
‏ت. أنالستبأحسنحاللأننيحزينة
‏ث. كيفحالكأناطيبيشكرا
‏ج. مرحبااسميمحمدوأنابخير
‏ح. صباحالخيراسميشعيبوأناطيب

6. Fill in the grid with the information in English

	Name	Age	Emotion
e.g.	*Yusuf*	*8*	*Happy*
a.	Ibrahim		
b.	Maryam		
c.	Hasan		
d.	Khalid		
e.	Aisha		

7. Spot the Intruder:

Identify the word in each sentence the speaker is NOT saying

مثال: أنا بخير، <u>شكرا</u>!

ا. مساء الخير، أنا طيب، مرتاح ومبتهج

ب. صباح مساء الخير، أنا جيد جدا

ت. أنا بأحسن حال لأنني لست هادئ

ث. مرحبا، أنا لست بأحسن حال أبدا لأنني متعبة

ج. كيف حالك؟ أنا بخير جدا

8. Faulty Echo:

Identify and underline the word in Arabic that is pronounced incorrectly in each sentence

مثال: <u>مرحبا</u>، أنا بخير

ا. صباح الخير أنا طيب

ب. أنا بأحسن حال لأنني سعيدة

ت. أنا بخير لأنني مرتاحة

ث. كيف حالك؟ أنا طيب

ج. أنا لست بأحسن حال لأنني حزين

ح. أنا بخير لأنني مبتهج

خ. مساء الخير، أنا لست بأحسن حال

9. Narrow Listening - Gap-fill

ا. مرحبا، أنا ـــــــ لأنني مبتهج	بخير
ب. صباح الخير، أنا بأحسن حال لأنني ـــــــ	مضغوط
ت. ـــــــ الخير، أنا لست بأحسن حال لأنني ـــــــ	شكرا
ث. كيف حالك؟ أنا طيبة، ـــــــ	سعيد
ح. كيف حالك؟ أنا ـــــــ ولكنني متعب	صباح
	طيب

THE LANGUAGE GYM

Unit 9. I can greet and say how I am: VOCAB BUILDING

1. Match Up

a. Relaxed — ا. متعب

b. How are you? — ب. مرتاحة

c. Calm — ت. أنا

d. Happy — ث. حزين

e. Tired — ج. متوترة

f. I am — ح. هادئ

g. Cheerful — خ. سعيدة

h. Nervous — د. مبتهج

i. Sad — ذ. كيف حالك؟

a	b	c	d	e	f	g	h	i

2. Broken Words

Happy — ا.سـ ـــــــــ

Fine — ب. بخـ ـــــ

Stressed — ت. مـ ــــــ

Good — ث. طـ ـــ

Good morning — ج. صبـ ـــ ا ـــــــ

Thanks — ح. شـ ــــــ

Because — خ. لأ ـــــ

I am — د. أ ـــ

Well — ذ. بأ ـ حـ ــــ

3. Complete with the missing words

I am well because I am **happy**.	ا. أنا بأحسن حال لأنني ـــــــ
I am not well because I am tired.	ب. أنا ـــــ بأحسن حال لأنني متعبة
I'm good **because I am** cheerful.	ت. أنا طيب ـــــ مبتهج
I'm **sad**.	ث. أنا ـــــــ
How **are you?** I am fine because I am **relaxed**	ج. كيف ـــــ ؟ أنا بخير لأنني ـــــــ

حزين	لست	سعيدة	حالك	لأنني	مرتاح

THE LANGUAGE GYM

Unit 9. I can greet and say how I am: READING

1. Sylla-bees
Translate the phrases putting the cells in the correct order

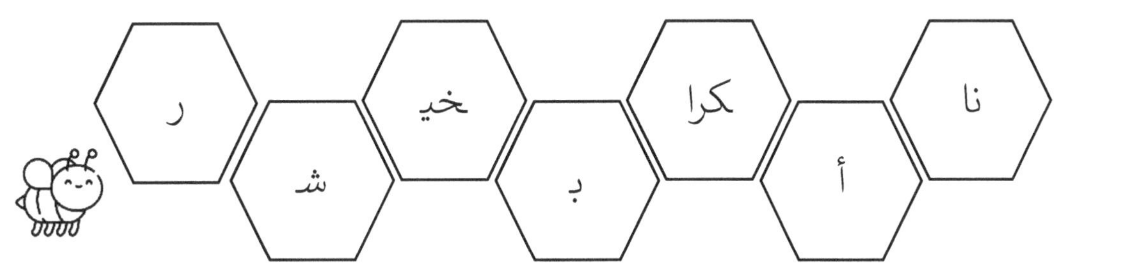

a. *I'm fine, thank you.*

أ__بـ__، شـ_______.

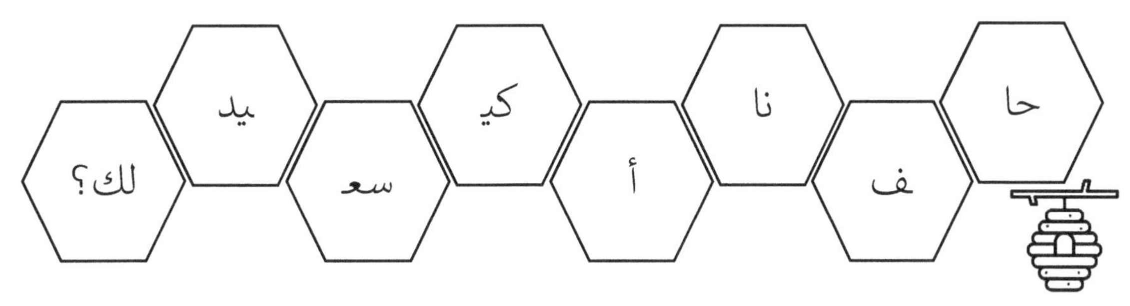

b. *How are you? I'm happy.*

ك_______ حـ_______؟ أ____ سـ_______.

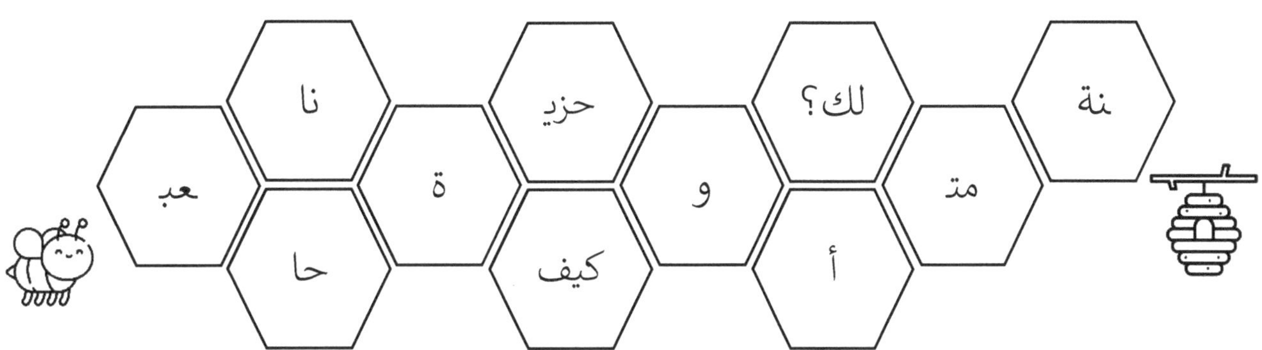

c. *How are you? I'm tired and sad (f).*

ك_______ حـ_______؟ أ___ مـ_______ و_______.

THE LANGUAGE GYM

	Name	Age	Feeling	Reason
e.g.	Ibrahim	8	good	cheerful
a.				
b.				
c.				
d.				
e.				

THE LANGUAGE GYM

1. Spelling

a. I am fine.

ا. أ __ __ بـ __ ______

b. I am good.

ب. __ ناط__بـ

c. Because I am happy.

ت. لـ __ني سـ ـيـ ـة

d. Because I am sad.

ث. لأنـ __ ـزيـ ____

e. Because I am relaxed.

ج. __ني ـرتـ __

f. How are you?

ح. كيـ __ حـ ـلـ __؟

g. I am not well.

ح. أنا __ـسـ __ بأحـ ____ حـ __ ل

2. Anagrams – Remember to join the letters correctly!

a. م ت و ت ر ن أ أ.   *I am nervous.*

b. م ر م ي ا ي س م.   *My name is Maryam.*

c. أ ن أ   ض م ط و غ.   *I am stressed.*

d. س ة ع د ي أ ن أ س ل ت.   *I am not happy.*

e. ح ب أ س ن ل ح ا ن أ أ.   *I am well.*

3. Faulty Translation
Spot the difference and correct the English

I am tired	I am _cheerful_	مثال: أنا متعب
	I am happy	ا. أنا طيب
	What's your name?	ب. كيف حالك؟
	I am nervous	ت. أنا مرتاح
	I am sad	ث. أنا حزين
	I am fine, however I am cheerful	ج. أنا بخير لأني مبتهج

4. Phrase-level Translation.
How would you say it in Arabic?

a. I am well. ____ 

b. I am not well.____

c. How are you? ____

d. I am relaxed. (m) ____

e. I am stressed. (m) ____

f. I am cheerful. (f)____

g. Hello, I am good. ____

h. I am calm. (f) ____

i. I am nervous. (f)____

No Snakes No Ladders

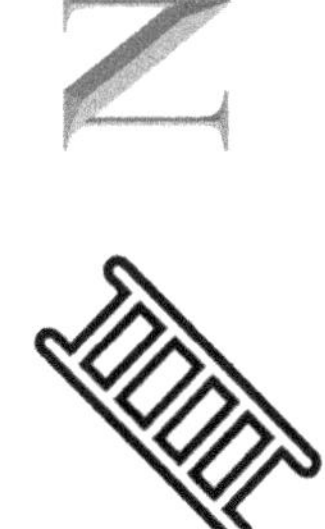

خروج	15 لأني مرتاحة	16 عمري عشر سنوات	وصول
1 مرحبا	14 عمري ثماني سنوات	17 أنا متعب	30 ليلة سعيدة
2 اسمي	13 كم عمرك؟	18 أنا بأحسن حال	29 عمري أربع سنوات
3 اسمي مريم	12 عمري إحدى عشرة سنة	19 مساء الخير	28 أنا طبيب
4 ما اسمك؟	11 عمري تسع سنوات	20 عمري خمس سنوات	27 اسمي حسن
5 صباح الخير	10 لأني متعب	21 لأني هادئة	26 أنا بخير
6 اسمي إبراهيم	9 أنا مضغوط	22 عمري سبع سنوات	25 أنا عمري اثنا عشرة سنة
7 ٩	8 عمري ست سنوات	23 شكرا	24 مرحبا، أنا لست بأحسن حال

THE LANGUAGE GYM

No Snakes No Ladders

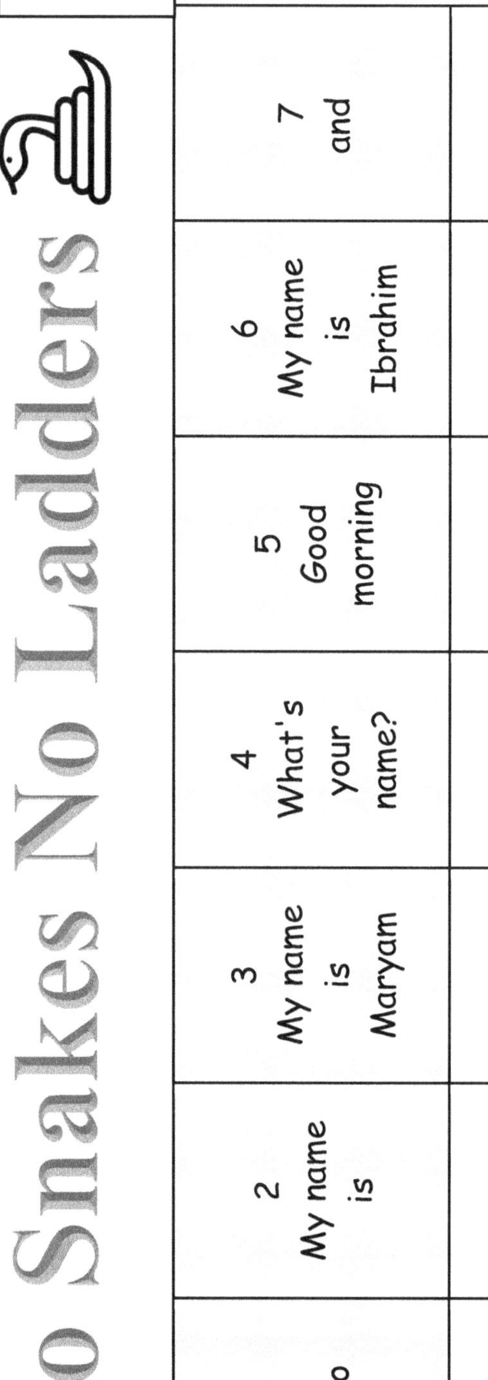

START

FINISH

1 — Hello

2 — My name is

3 — My name is Maryam

4 — What's your name?

5 — Good morning

6 — My name is Ibrahim

7 — and

8 — I am 6 years old

9 — I am stressed (m)

10 — Because I am tired (m)

11 — I am 9 years old

12 — I am 11 years old

13 — How old are you?

14 — I am 8 years old

15 — Because I am relaxed (f)

16 — I am 10 years old

17 — I am cheerful (m)

18 — I am well

19 — Good afternoon

20 — I am 5 years old

21 — Because I am calm (f)

22 — I am 7 years old

23 — Thank you

24 — Hello, I am not well

25 — I am 12 years old

26 — I am fine

27 — My name is Hasan

28 — I am good (m)

29 — I am 4 years old

30 — Good evening

THE LANGUAGE GYM

UNIT 9 – ANSWERS - I can greet and say how I am

LISTENING

1. Listen and tick the word you hear

ا. طيب   ب. هادئ   ت. مبتهج   ث. بأحسن حال   ج. مضغوط

2. Listen and add the correct vowels

د. مَرْحَبا، اِسْمِيْ مُوْسَى	ا. أَنَا مُبْتَهِج
ذ. أَنَا جَيِّدٌ جِدًّا	ب. لَيْلَة سَعِيْدَة
ر. صَبَاحُ الْخَيْرِ	ت. أَنَا هَادِئ
ز. أَنَا طَيِّب	ث. مَسَاءُ الْخَيْر
س. أَنَا مُرْتَاحَة	ج. أَنَا بِأَحْسَنِ حَال
ش. أَنَا مُتَوَتِّر	ح. أَنَا حَزِيْن
ص. أَنَا مَضْغُوْظ	خ. أَنَا مُتْعَبَة

3. Complete with the missing syllables in the box below

ا. أنا مضغوط   ب. انا جيد   ت. صباح الخير   ث. مساءالخير   ج. أنا لست بأحسن حال

ح. أنا بخير لأني سعيدة   خ. أنا مبتهج   د. مرحبا، اسمي عمر   ذ. أنا متعب

ر. أنا لست بأحسن حال لأني متوتر

4. Listen and choose the correct spelling

1. صباح الخير   **2.** أنا   **3.** مساء الخير   **4.** متعبة   **5.** بخير

6. سعيد   **7.** مضغوط   **8.** حزين   **9.** كيف حالك؟   **10.** هادئ

5. Break the flow: Separate the words and write out the sentences correctly underneath

ا. أنابخيرلأنني مبتهج

ب. أنالست بأحسن حال لأني متعبة

ت. مرحبا أنا لست بأحسن حال لأني حزينة

ث. كيف حالك أناطيب شكرا

ج. مرحباسمي محمدوأنابخير

ح. صباح الخير اسمي شعيب وأنا طيب

6. Fill in the grid with the information in English

1. Yusuf 8 Happy 2. Ibrahim 10 Sad 3. Maryam 7 cheerful 4. Hasan 5 calm
5. Khalid 12 nervous 6. Aisha 9 stressed

7. Spot the Intruder
ا. مرتاحة ب. مساء ت. لست ث. أبدا ج. جدا
8. Faulty Echo
ا. طيب ب. سعيدة ت. بخير ث. كيف ج. مبتهج ح. مساء
9. Narrow Listening - Gap-fill
ا. مرحبا، أنا **طيب** لأني مبتهج (طيب)
ب. صباح الخير، أنا بأحسن حال لأني **سعيد(سعيد)**
ت. صباح الخير ، أنا لست بأحسن حال لأني **مضغوط(مضغوط)**
ث. كيف حالك؟ أنا طيبة، **شكرا (شكرا)**
ج. كيف حالك؟ أنا **بخير** ولكني متعب (بخير)

Unit 9. I can greet and say how I am: VOCAB BUILDING
1. Match Up
1. ب   2. ذ   3. ح   4. خ   5. ا   6. ت   7. د   8. ج   9. ث
2. Broken Words

ا. سعيد ب. بخير ت. مضغوط ث. طيب ج. صباح الخير ح. شكرا خ. لأني د. أنا ذ. بأحسن حال

3. Complete with the missing words
ا. **سعيد** ب. **لست** ت. **لأني** ث. **حزين** ج. **حالك**؟ ، حمرتاح

Unit 9. I can greet and say how I am: READING
1. Sylla-bees

Translate the phrases putting the cells in the correct order
ا. أنا بخير، شكرا   ب. كيف حالك؟ أنا سعيد   ت. كيف حالك؟ أنا متعبة و حزينة

2. Read the sentences and complete the grid below in English .

Reason	Feeling	Age	Name	
cheerful	fine	8	Ibrahim	e.g.
happy	good	11	Fatima	ا.
relaxed	well	13	Bilal	ب.
tired	not well	6	'Aisha	ت.
calm	fine	9	Maryam	ث.
nervous	not well	12	Sulaimaan	ج.

Unit 9. I can greet and say how I am: WRITING

1.

a.	I am fine.	ا. أنا بخير
b.	I am good.	ب. أنا طيب
c.	Because I am happy.	ت. لأني سعيدة
d.	Because I am sad.	ث. لأني حزين
e.	Because I am relaxed.	ج. لأني مرتاح
f.	How are you?	ح. كيف حالك؟
g.	I am not well.	ح. أنا لست بأحسن حال

2. Anagrams - Remember to join them correctly!

a. I am nervous أنا متوتر   b. my name is Maryam اسمي مريم

c. I am stressed أنا مضغوط   d. I am not happy أنا لست سعيدة   e. I am well أنا بأحسن حال

3. Faulty Translation. Spot the difference and correct with English words

ا. أنا طيب - I am tired   ب. كيف حالك؟ - How are you?   ت. أنا مرتاح – I am relaxed
ث. أنا حزين – I am sad   ج. أنا بخير لأني مبتهج – I am fine because I am cheerful

4. Phrase-level Translation. How would you say it in Arabic?

a. أنا بأحسن حال

b. أنا لست بأحسن حال

c. كيف حالك؟

d. أنا مرتاح

e. أنا مضغوط

f. أنا مبتهجة

g. مرحبا، أنا طيب

h. أنا هادئة

i. أنا متوترة